By GERALD DAWE

CATCHING THE LIGHT

Views & Interviews

GERALD DAWE

Salmon

Published in 2008 by
Salmon Poetry,
Cliffs of Moher, County Clare, Ireland
Website: www.salmonpoetry.com
Email: info@salmonpoetry.com

Copyright © Gerald Dawe, 2008

ISBN 978-1-903392-90-4

Cover image: Digital painting by Stasys Eidiejus
Author photograph: Amelia Stein
Cover design & typesetting: Siobhán Hutson

For my sister, Pamela

Acknowledgments

Thanks and acknowledgements are due to the following for permission to reprint material in this book:

'Ins & Outs', *Journal of Irish Studies*, (XIX, 2004).

'A Giant at my Shoulder: in Conversation with Marian Richardson', *RTE Radio* (April 30th, 1999)

'Moon's Corner': 'Special Issue on Thomas Kilroy', *Irish University Review*, (32:1, spring/summer 2002) and *New Hibernia Review* (11:1, spring 2007).

Niall McGrath, 'Catching the Light', *Honest Ulsterman* (100, 1995); revised version, *Black Mountain Review 11* (Spring/summer 2005)

John Brown, *In the Chair* (Cliffs of Moher, Salmon Publishing, 2002)

Katrina Goldstone, 'Twilight Zones', *Irish Studies Review* 13:2 (May 2005)

Alan Titley, 'The Poet's Chair', *Poetry Ireland Archive*, (September, 2003) Transcription: Proprietary work by the John J. Burns Library, Boston College, Chestnut Hill, Massachusetts, 02467 U.S.A., 2007, 617-552-3282, transcribed by Lindsay Haney and Sarah Nytroe, supervisor Elizabeth Sweeney.

Nicholas Allen & David Gardiner, 'The Way It Is', *An Sionnach* 3:1 (Spring 2007)

'The War Next Door', *Irish Pages* (Spring/Summer 2003).

Poems by Gerald Dawe are published by The Gallery Press.

Other extracts were published in *The Irish Times*, *Metre*, *Poetry Ireland Review* and *Fortnight Magazine* and broadcast on RTÉ and BBC Northern Ireland. Acknowledgements are also due to my friends and colleagues in the School of English, Trinity College Dublin, to Culture Ireland and The British Council for their support. The author would also like to particularly thank Caroline Walsh for her encouragement and ideas and Lilian Foley for all her help in preparing this book for publication.

Contents

'There is something illusionistic and illusory about the relationship of time and space as we experience it in travelling, which is why whenever we come home from elsewhere we never feel quite sure if we have really been abroad'.

—W G Sebald, *Austerlitz* (2001)

I

Ins and Outs

Some lines of poetry remain fixed in one's mind and they can surface at any time. Two poems have stayed with me in this way. They come from my years at Orangefield Boys' School, Belfast during the mid-1960s. I can still hear the voice of my first teacher of English, Mr. Dai Francis, recite the General Prologue to the *Canterbury Tales*, as the class looked on, caught somewhere between awe and embarrassment:

> Whan that Aprille with hise shoures sote
> The droghte of March hath perced to the rote,
> And bathed every veyne in swich licour
> Of which vertu engendred is the flour.

We would have been about fifteen years' old at the time. The other set of lines is from the opening of another great English poem:

> Him the Almighty Power
> Hurled headlong flaming from the ethereal sky
> With hideous ruin and combustion down
> To bottomless perdition, there to dwell
> In adamantine chains and penal fire.

The voice this time is Sam McCready, and he is putting the fifth and sixth years through a rehearsal of his dramatisation of Milton's *Paradise Lost*, a set text for the 'A' level English in the 1960s. Orangefield was an extraordinary school, managed by the great, enlightened educationalist, John Malone in the heartland of east Belfast. I travelled weekdays across town from north Belfast, meeting friends outside C&As or Robinson Cleaver's, before taking the bus up the Albertbridge and Newtownards roads to Castlereagh. In English class we were also taught Keats and Shakespeare, Tennyson and Wilfred Owen. Our history was mostly economic and military, our geography global and geological; our sense of who we were based exclusively on the industrial and commercial city of Belfast.

Belfast was a country all to itself, and everything we knew and experienced was seen through the eyes of that needle. I dare say this exclusive, insular confidence, so much a part of the mid-60s, was a fool's paradise, but it was out of that time that I discovered poetry. I lived in the Public Library, visited bookshops and eagerly read everything I could get my hands on. There were a couple of good bookshops around Belfast in those days as well as Smithfield, in which you could stumble upon just about any book imaginable. Two anthologies of the time stand out though: Michael Roberts, *The Faber Book of Modern Verse*, another 'A' level set text and *The New Poetry*, edited by A. Alvarez, re-issued in 1966 with *Convergence*, a hypnotic Jackson Pollock as the cover. There was also the *Penguin Modern Poets Series* of which I was particularly taken by the great Russian poet Anna Akhmatova, the Sicilian Quasimodo, *Four Greek Poets* (Cavafy, Seferis, Elytis and Gatsos) and the Yugoslav, Vasko Popa. All this reading gave a young lad a great sense of the world beyond Belfast's walls.

Side by side with this life of books, there was the endless dancing, parties and concerts. I do not think anyone actually went anywhere, except, perhaps, for summer jobs to King's Lynn, Earl's Court or Guernsey. And there was the constant trafficking back and forth to London where, like thousands of other northern families of the time, part of my own family had emigrated in the early 1920s. As a bunch of young lads and girls we talked a lot and listened for what seemed like forever to R&B, Blues, jazz and 'High Pop' as the playwright Stewart Parker called it in his *Irish Times* column of the 1970s. The club-life in Belfast was vital and exciting. In the back of my mind, though, there was always the desire to write. I had already written some poems in school, recorded them in science notebooks alongside quotations from my favourite writers of the time—Albert Camus, Dostoyevsky, W. B. Yeats and Dylan Thomas. I showed the poems to a handful of friends, treating the whole thing like a terrible secret. Writing and poetry were deeply private, almost sacred, things to do, but there was also the nagging if subconscious question: how could someone from a background such as my own, actually write with any degree of confidence? What kind of English was the 'right' English to write in, anyway—the English spoken around me? Who would be bothered or interested, in the first place?

There were, along with the schoolbooks and the Penguins, several anthologies lying around the house, which my grandmother had used for elocution classes. I could hear the young hopefuls of our neighbourhood learn how to articulate and open their vowels, and listen to my grandmother tap out rhythms on the little baize table as the boys and girls faced themselves in the mirror. The sound of their voices moving in and out of performance (she also taught singing) had a strange effect on me. I became almost suspicious of 'language' and drawn more to the look of things and of how one can convey that in words. But the books my grandmother used came in very handy. They included the work of many English and American poets whose different voices sounded more in keeping with what I was after, a language that sounded closer to the way we said things. Then in 1968 or so, Stewart Parker gave a special class at which he read poems by Sylvia Plath. The shock was immediate and I will never forget the opening of 'Fever 103':

> Pure? What does it mean?
> The tongues of hell
> Are dull, dull as the triple
>
> Tongues of dull, fat Cerberus
> Who wheezes at the gate.

And from 'Daddy':

> There's a stake in your fat black heart
> And the villagers never liked you.
> They are dancing and stamping on you.
> They always *knew* it was you.
> Daddy, daddy, you bastard, I'm through.

My first published poem was called 'I'm Through' in honour of Sylvia Plath. Around this time, too, I sent to Michael Longley, through the sister of a friend who was being taught by him, a poem called 'From This Time Without'. The poem was based upon northerner Colin Blakely's performance in Denis Potter's television play, *The Son of Man*. Michael Longley wrote back to me with a priceless list of recommended English, American and Irish poets which I duly tracked down.

When I eventually went to college a couple of years after leaving school, I had behind me a lot of reading and a devotee's unwieldy sense of what literature meant. I also had a rather undisciplined idea that writing poetry, and writing about it, was what I wanted to do with my life. After a somewhat circuitous route (hesitation about drama school in London or art history in Sussex) I finally started at the fledgling New University of Ulster in 1971 with the left-wing English novelist and critic Walter Allen as professor. A mixed bunch of Irish (north and south), Scottish, English and some Americans beating the draft, held discussions in tutorials and late night sessions, in the unlikely setting of boarding rooms, rented flats and houses in what was known, in local parlance, as The Triangle—Portstewart, Coleraine and Portrush. Also during this time at the University of Ulster, I started to learn from friends, as much as in lectures, about Irish writing, in both languages. That was a revelation, to such an extent that I chanced my arm at writing a couple of plays in Irish and worked on their translation into Irish. That was 1973-74 and then I started postgraduate work on the Tyrone novelist and short story writer, William Carleton at University College Galway, ending up teaching there. I busied myself with various writing schemes, establishing the monthly literary supplement 'Writing in the West', published by the *Connacht Tribune* and organizing throughout the west writers' workshops called 'Starting to write'. I also published with Blackstaff Press my first book of poems, *Sheltering Places* in 1978.

There was a kind of naïveté about such things then that has, probably inevitably, given way to the increased professionalisation and marketing of Irish poetry both at home and abroad. The naïveté also extends in my case to the arbitrariness with which I took up teaching. Indeed I used to wake up in a cold sweat recalling my first class in 1977 (on Keats's poetry) when I had prepared enough material for a semester instead of just an hour. I can remember in the lecture hall half-full with uniformed army cadets, nuns and a scattering of young male clerics, a Christian Brother, returned from the Missions, sitting at the back of the class smiling indulgently at my crammed and rapid race against the clock and trying to get me to slow down the pace of delivery.

For much of the early 1980s I was sleep-walking, living and raising a family, and writing about the west of Ireland; learning about different styles of life and witnessing the saga of the north as it unfolded before a bewildered Republic. That story proved to be emblematic of what would happen elsewhere in Europe in the late 1980s and 1990s. But the crisis came in 1981 when the birth of our daughter crossed against the anguish and aftermath of the hunger strikes. Where I remembered the common ground of the pre-Troubles era and a determination *not* to bow to history's grand imperatives, there was now nothing but history, history being re-enacted and debated to what seemed no particular, defined and achievable political end. I felt I had to rethink. I began to tap discarded energies and return to the freer, eclectic roots that I had known growing up in Belfast and before the dark days had overtaken the city. I started to explore my own family's mixed roots, going back generations to European refugees coming into Ireland, setting up home here and the significance of that kind of unacknowledged difference. I was also intrigued by the history of writing in and about Belfast itself, about Protestantism and its influence on inherited attitudes to writers; and vice versa.

For the place of literature seemed to be on the leafy margins of the Belfast I knew growing up. Where we lived in north Belfast, for instance, there was so far as I could tell no writers: one painter (William Conor), an elocution teacher (my grandmother) and piano-instructress (my grandmother), but no writers. Then, one morning I saw a man in a very dapper trench coat with a large briefcase standing in the bus queue and recognised his face from a photograph in the *Belfast Telegraph*. My mother confirmed the rumour that he (Jack Wilson was his name) was a writer – of novels – and lived in a flat just up from our own house. He kept to himself and I had heard nothing about him until relatively recently when I discovered that he had died in 1997 at the age 60. His novels had been very well received when they were first published, in the 1960s. So far as I know they are mostly unavailable now with the exception of *The Wild Summer*, reissued by Lagan Press in 2001.

Music meant as much as writing. In fact it probably meant more, much more. If we were sulky know-it-alls, whose hero was Albert Camus, we loved hanging out at the City Hall, the Wimpy Bar or the Steps of either the Linen Hall Library or the Central Library in downtown Belfast. We listened to Van Morrison on the transistor radio and thought we saw him getting the Gilnahirk bus. We went for what seemed like every day and night to Sammy Huston's Jazz Club, the Maritime, Betty Staffs, or the Plaza in the afternoons and thought that world would never end. The bands played on and on and on. In 1966 it looked that way, at least. In only four years it was, of course, blown apart. As for poetry?

Much has understandably been made of the great generation of northern poets who published first and second collections in the early and mid Sixties, in particular those associated with Queen's University and who attended Philip Hobsbaum's writing workshops— Seamus Heaney, Michael Longley, Stewart Parker, among others. This 'group', supplemented by a younger generation of Queen's students in the late 1960s and early 1970s—Paul Muldoon, Ciaran Carson, Frank Ormsby, and Medbh McGuckian—would become identified worldwide by the late 1970s as the 'Northern Poets'. But like many aspiring poets of the time who did not attend Queen's I reckon the first time I heard of there being such a 'Belfast Group' was when I was well gone from the city and living in the west coast of Ireland. Which is not to say that individual names of the Group were unfamiliar. In or around 1967 the head prefect at Orangefield gave a special class on Seamus Heaney's *Death of a Naturalist* and we all sat around being very cool when he quoted:

Right down the dam gross-bellied frogs were cocked
On sods; their loose necks pulsed like sails. Some hopped:
The slap and plop were obscene threats. Some sat
Poised like mud grenades, their blunt heads farting.

For city-boys that was a bit of a culture shock. But whatever poetry was read during the 1960s in the Belfast I knew it wasn't Irish. In 1967, I bought *W H Auden: The Penguin Poets*, selected by the author, and as I've previously noted, our school text was the mind-bending *Faber Book of Modern Verse*, edited by Michael Roberts. The only Irish representation in the 1965 reprint of that anthology, used in classrooms up and down the length of Northern Ireland and the UK was W B Yeats and Louis MacNeice. While in Alvarez's *New Poetry*, again a very popular anthology of the time, there was not one Irish poet in the entire anthology—which goes to show not just how things were looking *before* the Northern impact but also the scale of the achievement *thereafter*.

The notion that there was a 'Group' of poets knocking around in the heart of Belfast discussing poetry would have seemed utterly remote. If you wrote, best to keep it secret or wait until the late night blackout in the front room when the pals were laid back and you could speak out of the darkness. After a brief spell in London, and on my return to Belfast, a few names started to circulate: Heaney, Longley and Mahon. But as to their constituting a group, never mind 'The Group', it did not penetrate deepest north Belfast. There may have been some sense that a group of poets from the north were publishing in London, and could be seen from time to time around the place; but this would have been after the event. Not being part of any literary scene, being turned on by music of the Sixties, obviously meant our minds were elsewhere. Whatever we read was more likely to come from America and England than from Ireland and it had to compete with the weekly order of *NME* (*New Musical Express*) and *Melody Maker*.

When 'Ireland' came into view, it was traditional music, not the poetry of any Group. Indeed, by the time I was a student at NUU, John Montague and Thomas Kinsella, James Simmons and Derek Mahon had a deeper presence. Be that as it may, the political warning systems were moving to full alert from about 1972, the year that Derek Mahon's *Lives* appeared. In that slimmest of slim volumes the non-Groupie seemed to get it dead-right from the perspective of a 20 year old student living on the chastening north east coast:

Spring lights the country; from a thousand
dusty corners, house by house,
from under beds and vacuum cleaners,
empty Calor Gas containers,
bread bins, car seats, crates of stout,
the first flies cry to be let out;
to cruise a kitchen, find a door
and die clean in the open air [.]

In time other names were added to the seedbed of 'The Group' and before long an extended poetic family came into critical being— the Northern Poets. It's probably true to say that without the idea of the 'Group', the notion of 'Northern Poetry' would be less peda- gogically convincing. It should be understood more as an extraor- dinary moment of literary achievement and historical coincidence than as an example of some kind of inherent cultural identity just waiting to happen. That kind of historical determinism strikes me as folly. The books of poems tell us as much: if one considers, for instance, the imaginative differences which distinguish, say, Michael Longley from Seamus Heaney, or Derek Mahon from both. There is, too, the temporary loss to view of Stewart Parker or the amnesia surrounding the role that Padraic Fiacc played in his Glengormley home encouraging many local and visiting poets and prose-writers during the late 1950s and early 1960s, and before him, John Hewitt, Roy McFadden, Sam Hanna Bell, John Boyd and so on. That complex literary and social history has yet to be written, along side the necessary critical discriminations.

For a teenager, living in the middle of a vibrant Sixties provincial city called Belfast, all this awareness was for the future, which of course is actually here and now. The poems I wrote back then were about nothing much but a young man's seeking refuge in 'language' only to discover that there is no such place. The poems were written in the attic bedroom of a quiet, tall, terrace house, full of women of various different backgrounds and the voices, of course, always the voices. It was a house on a main road with its back to the Cave Hill, looking out over Brantwood, Grove Park, Seaview, the Shore Road and the Lough—landscapes and interiors, unknown histories in very many ways, that slowly asserted themselves the further away I went from them.

A Giant at my Shoulder

What stands out in my mind is the house in which we lived in north Belfast. It overlooked the Lough and was a house full of women—my grandmother, my mother, my sister, my sister's friends, my mother's friends, and my grandmother's friends. My grandmother was a singer, a light opera singer, and she used to have these little soirées in the front room. She also taught elocution and the piano. So she would sing and then poems would have been recited by her pupils. I used to stand at the top of the stairs listening and it always fascinated me that there was a little theatre going on in the front room. It was always very well organized. It was good fun and they enjoyed themselves and they would leave happy. What struck me from a very early age (I would have been about five or six in the late Fifties) about the adult soirées she held at night, and at weekends, was their manner. Everything was contained—nothing ever got out of hand and even though they enjoyed themselves and you could hear the laughter, there was something reserved about it all. She would sing through the house the odd time but mostly she kept her voice to herself, so to speak.

Later on we had a record player in the front room and eventually my friends and I started to take over that space. My mother's record player was there and when her brother, my uncle, returned from the R.A.F he brought with him some records by people like

Lester Young, George Shearing and Ella Fitzgerald. I used to hear Ella being played on that gramophone: another woman's voice to join all the rest of them. And then one night, (I was about nine, maybe ten), Ella Fitzgerald played Belfast. I remember my mother coming back in—she went out to that 'gig' with our next door neighbour, an Austrian woman,—and she was very excited and told me it was just an extraordinary experience to see Ella Fitzgerald there on stage singing. The funny little comment that she made ("I'm sent") stuck in my mind—clearly she was rocking and rolling in the aisles, not quite but almost. Our next-door neighbour was rather austere about such displays, I imagine, as she was a very private woman who had endured quite a lot during the WWII in Vienna. My mother's enthusiasm for actually listening to this music moved on to me and from quite an early age I was turned on to this kind of jazz. So what I remember most about those days in the Fifties was a kind of underground feeling. I'm sure there were houses throughout Belfast where this kind of interest was being shown and people were into it in a big way.

The parallel that comes to mind is that when I was eavesdropping as a kid in the late Fifties there must have been an adult generation who had done something similar a decade before when all these army guys had returned from the war. They had been stationed in Germany, listening to American music and there had been a whole series of army installations in Northern Ireland. Black guys stationed there must have been playing music. They'd go down to the Plaza ballroom in Belfast; they'd have been dancing down there, too. So the music was very much part of the environment in the Belfast that I grew up in. It was a series of so many different kinds of music but the one that seemed to have an impact was the 'subversiveness' of jazz. This moved by the early Sixties to a group of little clubs springing up around the town where R&B, soul, and Tamla Motown were played. A bridge was made between the likes of Ella Fitzgerald, Lester Young that I was hearing in the late Fifties and then, ten years later, the friends I had in my mid-teens, started to get into R&B and blues. But the one voice, the one name, that summoned all that up for us was Van Morrison and Them. There were other very good bands around at that time I'm talking about in the mid-Sixties, very good bands, like The Few, The Interns, Sam Mahood and the Just Five and so on. There were bands playing it seemed every night. I do remember very clearly the sense that we had as young teenagers that we didn't go into the pop stuff so much. It was R&B—and then someone like Jimi Hendrix Experience was very big with us.

Belfast was still available then, everybody lived in the city, there wasn't a sense of being ghettoized or from neighbourhoods that you couldn't move in and out of, the city centre was a home for everybody and it had a marvelous energy to it. There would be dances on a Wednesday night, Friday night, Saturday afternoon, Saturday night, and even Sunday. Everybody just went dancing. I remember around the side of the City Hall, one afternoon in late spring, the weather was good and somebody had a transistor on and we were lying on the grass and we heard Van Morrison with Them, 'Here comes the Night' and that song became a theme-tune, a hymn. When I started to go to the Maritime (where Them had played) it had changed name and was called Club Rado. So I never saw Them live on stage, though I did hear Morrison on the tiny stage of Sammy Houston's Jazz Club performing Dylan's, 'Like a Rolling Stone', with Frankie Connolly and the Styx, a rare combination for sure.

What I do recall very clearly is the energy in Van Morrison's voice, a very Belfast voice. That somebody could get up on stage and sing with the accent you heard in the streets—like you sang at a bus stop—was unimaginable. To think that here was a guy who was from Belfast, who was on 'Ready Steady Go' and that Them as a band were doing very well over in Britain and the odd time, you'd see him around town, was a great source of unexpressed pride.

In those days there wasn't the hype or the self-consciousness about that there is now. Them with Van Morrison gave voice to a generation. I don't want to put too much on it, but in those days we'd have had little idea really about sectarianism or anything like that. It just wasn't part of the psychic landscape. I used to date girls from the top of the Falls Road, and we'd walk home together. You used to walk everywhere. Everybody used to meet in the clubs; so he captured that defiance in his voice and the sort of aggression of Them that—"We're here"—a kind of dismissiveness, publicly, of being in 'the business'—the music business. I know now that they had to fight their corner.

I can imagine some would have been badly treated by 'the industry' but Morrison stood for a kind of independence. We wouldn't have been conscious of this at the time but certainly there was the sense in which he was doing his thing and then just moving on. It wasn't as if he was being a 'pop star'—that just wasn't there at all. This music was something he could 'do', that he was brilliant at. He'd get on stage with the band and then go. In a way he was an anti-hero. Them were anti-heroes and they fitted the mood. But it wouldn't have been a conscious thing, a pose. He then became more sophisticated.

We tried different things and in Smithfield—which was a place, like a casbah, where you could buy and sell just about anything, including records, second hand records, you'd get anything you wanted. It was all second hand. It was magnificent—coins, clothes, old transistor radios, wardrobes, you name it—and there was one shop, whose name won't come to mind now, and the guy who had this shop was very much interested in music, soul music, R&B and blues.

I will never forget going in. Now to see this guy you'd think he would be looking under the bonnet of a car, but when he started to talk about blues, R&B, you were in some other territory. He knew everything: different versions of the same songs—exactly who was who in the States. We used to go in and talk and he put on a track—it was a Chess album track of John Lee Hooker. We were all in the shop (it was just a big counter and the records were stacked behind it) and that was just extraordinary to hear this guy and that then took us down another route. The thing to remember is that there was the feeling then that music was the counter culture. Belfast was very much a city dominated by work—that is what you were there for—work, work, work.

When I think of the 1960's, the energies that were around were very much directed at getting out and about; getting into Belfast. What personified this feeling of being able to express yourself 'here' was a Belfast band doing very well. They suggested to those of us who we were about six or seven years younger at the time that you *could* do these things, not to be afraid, to set up our own band. We did; it was a band called The Trolls!

We played in different places. We were pretty desperate. I think we lasted about six months and that was it. But it was the kind of confidence that Them gave that myself and, a few others I knew, started to write. We realized we weren't singers, we weren't musicians, but we could move into other 'art forms', if you like. In that sense, Van Morrison opened the door for myself and other young men and women to think that 'work' wasn't the only way forward, that there was a different *kind* of work and you could do it on the stage or with a pen. It was the possibilities, which Them generated that was so important. He broke the sound barriers of what was often an uptight, class-bound society, too. By the late Sixties when Them had broken up Morrison was really on his way out as he'd gone over to the States. We lost sight of him but then he produced the album, which everybody recognises and identifies as being so extraordinary—*Astral Weeks*. The thing to remember is that Belfast was just on the cusp of a whole series of marches. The Civil Rights movement was up and going.

A lot of pals had left Belfast and where now in London or they'd disappeared elsewhere. When *Astral Weeks* came out there were just a few of us still around. To listen to the kind of organization of that album, the sense of it being a huge poetic shift away from the raucous energies of Them, pointed in another direction too—which was actually into poetry. For the mood poem that is *Astral Weeks*—I mean the entire album but particularly "Beside You", was so revealing. Here was this strong voice—strong personality—that yet could also move across into something so much more lyrical and moody. That was a big shift, too. You can be a Belfast guy and you can be lyrical! It seems silly now but that shocked people, the extent to which Morrison had moved across into another mode, another mood. Then of course the curtain fell with 'The Troubles' and by about 1970, '71, '72 it seemed as if *Astral Weeks*, Them and all that, were light years ago.

My feeling of it now is that Morrison's music 'disappeared' in the sense that the immediacy of what was happening in Belfast (the terrorism, the darkness) overtook us. We seemed to lose out, we all broke up and the 'gang' drifted apart and gone our different ways. I went to college in Coleraine and then eventually moved out of the North altogether to Galway. So the joy, the pleasure and the energy that Morrison embodied went underground as the very heavy political charge of the Seventies took over. It was only later on that I heard 'Listen to the lion' from the magnificent, *It's too late to stop now*, a double album of his tour with the Caledonian Soul Orchestra. What you had was somebody who could literally lift the roof and bring together these totally different kinds of music. You had the energy of the voice, the dynamic quality there, and that marked an entire period for me really. That was Van Morrison at the time, doing his thing and not being compromised by 'Pop'. You had the feeling that he was going to produce something quite different.

The other thing that comes to my mind too is that we had a sense of being from Belfast. We didn't really have a sense of being 'Irish' as such. When you think about it, great bands used to come to Belfast—John Mayall, Hendrix, Cream, the Small Faces, and Pink Floyd. We didn't have to go to them. In a way we were almost arrogant about music. The kind of standards that we were used to was phenomenal so it created an expectation to which *all* other things had to measure up. What is inescapable about this time was that we really had such a marvelous experience *in* Belfast. Occasionally you'd get some old guy shouting something at you and there was always a little bit of tension on the periphery of life, but we had a marvelous time and it lasted until about 1970—the dancing, the music, the parties, moving throughout Belfast freely. By 1971-72, that had gone, more or less. When I returned home, the music seemed underground. It felt like we were old men talking about a period thirty years before instead of being only a few years before. There was definitely a shift.

'The Troubles' put into quarantine those kinds of energies but maybe they are re-surfacing, thirty years later. I don't know. I can't stress enough the importance of Morrison's own presence in the clubs and the kind of example he set when he moved outside Belfast. I think he ran out of space in Belfast. He'd done all he wanted to do there and he had to go somewhere else. Perhaps it's not sufficiently recognized that that was a huge step for someone to take in those days—a tremendously courageous thing to do—to move from Belfast and to head over to New York, not knowing what was going to happen. Without overdoing it, that was a remarkable achievement. It's okay now, moving here, there, and everywhere; there are huge resources available now. But in 1966, 1967, 1968 that was a big achievement and of course it paid off, because without the move you probably wouldn't have had *Astral Weeks*. He had been writing some of those lyrics in Belfast but you wouldn't have had the *quality* of that magnificent album, without the shift and the risk of moving to America and taking on extraordinary responsibilities there for such a young man.

By the late 1970s, there were other clubs, in the districts, in local neighbourhoods, where people went but the notion of Belfast itself, as being open and available, that had certainly gone. The violence had put paid to that. I remember very clearly walking through the town one night—it would've been about 1972 or '73—and it was like walking through a ghost town. We're forgetting these things and maybe it's no bad thing. The pubs shut at about 6pm or 7, the cinemas were closed and the buses stopped early. It was almost like you were walking through a city at war with itself. People literally withdrew into their own districts and then, inside their own districts, back into their own homes; they didn't look out. It was pretty bleak. I then left and moved to the west of Ireland and picked up, as I said, on Morrison again, with *It's too late to Stop Now*.

During the 1980's I'd been fiddling around with poems in Galway. I remember very clearly the sense that I had that I wanted to write *about* the background that I'd come from, but I wasn't too sure how to go about it. Then Morrison's example kicked in very strongly and the fact that he'd written about places, the streets and avenues of Belfast that I myself knew. It was almost as if a light went on and I found myself writing a whole sequence of poems about Belfast. I probably wouldn't have got to those without Van Morrison, in the way in which he had 'authorized' the ability to write about your own place. It's difficult to think now about the extent to which Belfast had been perceived as being 'anti-art', that you couldn't write poems out of that place.

Yet here was this guy who was singing songs and making music, hymns to places in Belfast that I knew well. I published *The Lundys Letter* (1985) and in that there are a number of poems about Belfast and its environs. I think it's very much down to Van Morrison's example, among one or two poets whose work I greatly admired. The other thing that strikes me about his music and influence is that he always is able to move in and out of different kinds of forms. He tapped into a form of expression which drew on poets like Blake, and at the same time, brought together some of the Beat poets.

There's a freedom in what he does and that's very exhilarating for a poet. We can get bogged down on very narrow gauges, but

Morrison's ability to blend, mix and draw on different kinds of energy and generate writing out of his own self, that was really 'empowering', as they say now, enabling, very striking.

Towards the end of the 1980's Van Morrison was planning a programme on poetry and music [*Coney Island of the Mind*, Channel 4, 1991] and I was involved. It was quite exciting to be with him and we'd a lot of laughs. We traveled around east Belfast, going to Orangefield—the school that Van Morrison went to and I went to as well. Being with him around that almost 'sacred' environment—the streams, the mountains, the hillside, the whole area—was really exciting. I also realized the extent to which he was an artist who had very strong commitment to the place, but also to a vision. It wasn't as if he was just literally documenting this area. He has a very powerful sense of how ordinary life is suffused with the *spirit* of place and, besides the fun that we had, it was intriguing to be with him as he walked through this area that he had done so much to praise through his music.

When you add everything up, Van Morrison's voice is absolutely distinct and unique. It's like having a presence that is un-moveable and totally committed to his art. And that's so refreshing, in this day and age, when people market themselves and put themselves into little slots, little niches. Morrison is just himself and he does exactly what he wants to do and he's got total commitment to that.

The sense that you had in Belfast in the 1950's was that everybody had to be in his or her own place; everything was correct; things were in their spot. Music was the way to break out of that and there was the feeling that you could get out of that control. That was the thing I loved about it. By the mid- 60's, Van Morrison, Them and others, were breaking through and transgressing that code, just by the sheer energy of their voices and music.

Morrison's music will live forever. There are so many magnificent albums from *Astral Weeks* to the present. Morrison's music will always 'be there' for one basic reason—that he sets out on a journey and he makes a bold sort of statement. The music is not constrained. You can move backwards and forwards through all these different forms and that's an important lesson and a fantastic example to have.

Moon's Corner

i

When I visited Galway the second time I stayed. In those days of the early 1970s, no one quaffed water from designer bottles but the bus driver used to stop, along with his passengers, at a pub in Roscommon for a couple of pints (and a whisky) before resuming the cross-border journey from Belfast to Galway. There was a border then too. Gardai, Irish defence forces, U.D.R., British soldiers, R.U.C., Customs and Excise men, and various others, whom we probably didn't see, peered out of makeshift roadside bunkers. It was a furtive time, five years of killing, bombings, reprisals, and assassinations, the razing of streets, riots, and looting, political crisis. Madness was in the air. No one really thought it would all become a way of life but in the café in Cavan (passengers changed bus services there, from Ulsterbus to C.I.E.) it felt as if life had not altered terribly much over the generations of tea and sandwiches, knowing nods and silent recognitions. But buses were now being hijacked, set on fire, stopped and searched, re-routed and bus stations had taken on a haunted, frightened aspect, surreptitiously at first and then, after the appalling destruction of Oxford Street Station in Belfast by Provo bombers, it was more than fear caught hold of glances. That bag? That box? That bicycle? That car?

When the bus pulled in alongside the steps to Eamon Ceainnt Station that mid-October I felt a dizzy sense of freedom. Freedom from the dark streets of home, freedom from the ceaseless rant and rancour; freedom from the closing down of the city in which I had grown up; freedom from the thugs and bullies. There was also a feeling of having escaped, just in the nick of time. The Belfast I had left behind was of a very confused summer that included doing final university exams during the Ulster Workers' Council strike, juking through UDA barricades; several months working in the Central Library and moving across the deserted city at night to the small flat I shared with an American pal in an east Belfast estate.

Eyre Square had an autumnal glow and a fresh breeze in the air. Back then the shape of the square had a very real sense of welcome to it. The houses, offices, hotels and shops seemed to set the tone for the rest of the townscape. I can't recall one tacky shop or hoarding. Many canals and bridges with high stone houses and warehouses, which, in those pre-tax incentive development days of the early 1970s, were roofless and windowless, made the city seem small and compact. I dumped my bag in the American Hotel and punctually headed to University College Galway, my first port of call, to introduce myself to my professor, Lorna Reynolds, and to the Dean, the classics scholar, 'Ma' Heavey.

The walk by Moon's Corner, the post office, down to the Law Court and Library and over the Salmon Weir Bridge, stays in my mind in slow motion. Everything was starkly etched in the late afternoon, livid with light. So when I turned into the Archway of U.C.G., Padraic O Flahertaigh, the Porter's answer to my query about directions to Aras de Brun, sounded equally bewitching.

I couldn't really believe my luck. Only a precarious few weeks prior, I had been stared at and finger-pointed and had taken foolish risks in the increasingly manic belief that Belfast was still an open city. My pal and I had been followed to our little flat in east Belfast. Loyalist paramilitaries had called to the door, "They're only collecting money, right?" I had worked my notice as a library assistant in the Fine Arts department of the Central Library in Belfast's Royal Avenue—bombs to the left of us, bombs to the right, scotch-taped windows left open wide, evacuation procedures, the bomb-disposal officer's hectoring voice on the megaphone, the resigned faces of we poor joe soaps standing waiting before we could resume our lives, 'after the bomb goes off'. Now I was walking towards the Arts Block, with the heavenly Corrib flowing by, my feet barely touching the ground.

As for Professor Reynolds, she was sitting in behind her desk, a tall spindly woman, wearing a Virginia Woolf-like hat, with an accent I couldn't quite locate. Cool but kind, formal yet interested, she asked how my journey had gone, had I found myself suitable accommodation, recommended I check out the Hardiman Library for its holdings in 19th century journals, newspapers, historical and literary texts, and that I should 'proceed to Kenny's' and see what I might find there.

A brief courtesy call with Prof. Heavey, a smiling adorable woman tending to plants in her office, and I was off again, skirting the canal, the Cathedral and into Nun's Island, passed the imagined home of Joyce's Gretta in 'The Dead', passed Dominick Street, over O Brien's Bridge, and into High Street, where on a corner, stood Tom Kenny's map shop, next door to Sonny Molloy's, which faced the double doors of Kenny's Bookshop, the front shop of which I entered with the jangle of a bell. From then on, for the next twenty years that is, Kenny's became home from home, with all its transformations and expansions—upstairs, downstairs, next door, towards Middle Street, the recall of the Abbeygate Street premises, the gallery in Salthill,—all these developments were logged alongside my own vague journey, from hotel to rented room in Spiddal to half a house in Knocknacarra to a flat in Abbeygate Street to a bungalow in Ballindooley on the Headford Road and finally to our home in Glenrevagh in Corrandula.

Kenny's was the backdrop; the fulcrum. My books were launched there, numbers of magazines edited were sent on their way; the walls of our different homes had paintings bought from Kenny's. Older artists were rediscovered, new friends made and met, strangers introduced, interviews conducted, photographs taken, luggage and messages left, drink consumed, rumours heard, first editions bought, borrowed, lost and found; afternoons spent 'perusing', evenings begun, weekends brokered, highlights installed in the memory, guests entertained, lives lived. 'Would you like some tea?' I turned from the bookshelves, William Carleton's *Traits and Stories of the Irish Peasantry* (two volumes, illustrations by Phiz) in my hand. 'Tea?' 'Yes, I always have a cup of tea around this time. Lemon tea. And you can borrow that if you like'. A rare edition. It was Mrs Kenny, a conductor, behind her bureau. A rare moment. A total stranger. Hooked for life. 'Yes, thanks' I said. 'Thanks' and told her briefly my story.

ii

A couple of years after that encounter, I met Tom Kilroy as he was preparing the ground for what was to become the inaugural Arts Council National Writers Workshop, which would be based at University College Galway. Tom as moderator was fascinated by what each of the individual writers, of whom I was one, could do with his or her own talent. He was unenamoured by ego and in those days the business of a writing career did not even arise as a question. Having given up full time teaching, Tom left no one in any doubt about the material rigours of the writing life. He was adamant that the only concern a writer should have was with the work; the private life was precisely that—private. Writing transformed all autobiography into something significantly different, or else it had failed to ignite as writing. As he said in an interview many years later: 'There is a kind of writing which repels me and that is the writing of easy sentiment or easy feeling, writing as a form of exhibitionism and sensational display'. The other thing I recall from those weekends in the old college was Tom's insistence on pushing each writer to the limit of what he or she was writing at the time and not to go for the accepted, acceptable thing. There was steeliness in his understanding of what made artistic sense, vigour to what merited serious attention, matched by his generosity about the vulnerability of 'it all'. His reading of classic and modern American and European writers sat lightly in all our discussions. When the term of workshops was over I realized that it had been a master class.

The west of Ireland was a very different place before the hectic unplanned redevelopment of Galway and its hinterlands. In many ways the county in the mid-1970s was as it had been for a century or more: an independent-minded, sophisticated, bilingual city-state on the edge of the country. It was a great place to be.

I wrote my thesis on William Carleton living in the heart of the city, in my girl's family's place in Mayo and in Ballyshrule where Tom and his sons lived in a rambling mill house in the middle of the countryside. A river ran through the grounds and there was an almost Chekhovian atmosphere to the place. Writers called. Books were discussed along with the latest theatre productions in Dublin, London, New York. Tom Mac Intyre brought word of Paris. Student days from Dublin in the Fifties and Sixties were recounted and the visits to the States. Sometimes it sounded as if William Faulkner, Flannery O Connor and Tennessee Williams lived up the road where discussions took place in the local pub about the latest GAA match or rugby international and (inevitably) what was happening in the North.

It was the greatest grounding into the cosmopolitan life of a very different kind of Ireland to that which so often appears as the present hyper-reality. I also started to write some poems there, which revisited the Belfast I had left and explored the Galway where I (mistakenly) thought I had just temporarily settled. The respect that Tom and his group of friends had for the life of the imagination, for ideas, was in stark contrast to the introverted and often complacent attitudes of the official southern scene. Of course, this robust respect stood out all the more against the horror of the northern 'Troubles' as it unfolded, day by day, week by week, into bloodshed and political collapse.

Our friendship developed out of those difficult years in the mid-to-late 1970s. When Tom eventually moved into Galway many leading writers visited to give readings in the college and town. He became a kind of magnet for younger writers, too, and for several of the by-now well-established theatre groups, all of whom thought highly of the independence of his ideas.

The committed position he held I saw as a passionately secular and a very rooted democratic republicanism that sees through the fug of Irish, or Northern Irish, self-obsession. It is a kind of uncommon, strong-minded social vision, which places responsibility for political and civic freedom squarely on the individual's shoulders to think and act for his or her self. He is in this sense a very political writer, probably the most political of his generation of writers in Ireland.

But to write about Tom means, of course, to write about Kilroy. It is impossible to separate our friendship from the plays and fiction and essays that he has written. There are the legendary performances from hearsay: Niall Toibin in *The Death and Resurrection of Mr. Roche*, Donal McCann in *Tea and Sex and Shakespeare*, Anna Massey and Alan Rickman in *The Seagull*. It was in the Peacock in 1977 that I first actually saw what Kilroy was about in that extraordinary play of his, *Talbot's Box*, with John Molloy in the lead role. When Molloy/Talbot is summoned from his death and stretches back into that torturous, bizarre and hilarious life on the stage, something clicked in my mind. This writer does not seek to console his audience; he wishes to challenge them. Ten years later in *Double Cross* when Stephen Rea as Lord Haw Haw rants on about his vision of human perfectibility, the chill factor shot through the auditorium of Derry's Guild Hall:

> All you earnest believers in the perfectibility of man, attend! When the first great fire burned, the ice melted and the monkey stood upright in that incredible heat of the young sun. His brain expanded in its box. Words came from his mouth. Words refined the hanging jaw. And the nose melted into its human proportion. When the second great fire comes man will be burned again out of his imperfection and into the shape of his dreams.

And when Bracken spills out his words, until exhaustion silences him, the surge of real dramatic energy was palpable. Ten years later again, in *The Secret Fall of Constance Wilde* in 1997, Jane Brennan's beautifully pitched innocent Constance darkens before our very eyes into a grandeur of understanding and a shocking vision of human acceptance. Kevin Flood's magisterial Sergeant in *Madame MacAdam's Travelling Theatre*, Gerard McSorley's compelling Narrator in Kilroy's version of Pirandello's *Six Characters in search of an Author*, Alan Devlin and Derbhla Crotty in the television play, *Gold in the Streets*, the radical and original innovation of *The Seagull* re-imagined in an Irish setting; of *Ghosts* as a contemporary morality play on AIDS. The plays have become part of our cultural self-awareness, anticipating, challenging, and reasserting the primacy of theatre as a form of artistic experience—tragic, comic, but always theatrical, and mindful of the audience's own emotional intelligence. This challenge provokes and destabilizes received opinion on what one should expect not just from 'theatre' but from 'Irish' theatre.

More than anything else Kilroy's plays seem visionary in the sense that they decry the impoverishment of human potential—political, moral, cultural—and the selling short of dramatic experience—of what happens when people gather to play. It is not only the language that counts but also the guiding, enfolding dramatic idea.

More than any other dramatist of the front rank, Kilroy's plays are about ideas. It is no surprise, therefore, that Kilroy's own ideas about writing and about the tradition of writing in Ireland should turn up new perspectives and new questions. His keynote lecture to the 1979 IASAIL (as it then was) conference at Maynooth, sticks out in my mind: 'I am fascinated [he was to state] and often appalled by what happens when the intense, concentrated hopes, fears and beliefs of the private person are subjected to the fragmenting, diffusionary effects of public life'. There is too the radical reading of the Irish theatrical tradition and particularly the place within it of the Anglo-Irish imagination, instalments of which we have been reading since the 1970s.

All this work looks like becoming a substantial, re-imagining of Irish writing since the eighteenth century: a kind of one-man literary revival. While the essays (and the reviews) play in and around the creative work as a testing ground, as sounding boards, the concentrated energy of Kilroy's writing life culminates in the as-yet unpublished play, *Blake*. It is a magnificent achievement. As he said, 'I don't think you can make any distinction between passion, feeling, the moral sensibility, and the ideas, which flow from that. They are all part of one. It's that network which I inhabit'.

Kilroy's fiction has had a curious life so far. From the trail-blazing success in 1971 of his novel, *The Big Chapel*—The Guardian Fiction Prize, Heinemann Award for Literature, Booker Prize shortlist, Irish Academy Prize—which established his name in the forefront of Irish and British novelists, *Angela*, a novel of sweeping emotional shifts and parodic intensities, remains unfinished; 'an abandoned work' to which he has only recently returned. The perversely interiorised, absent-minded, time-warped dream song of *Quirke* awaits its entrance. Such open-endedness is very much against the grain of the market-driven, managerial strategies of many contemporary careers. Perplexing, too, that Kilroy has not yet collected his own critical work such as the original writing on Yeats, Synge, O Casey, Beckett, Johnston and Friel. It points to the ongoing experimental nature of the man's writing and the integral part that his belief in the imagination as a freeing and undogmatic force, plays throughout all that he has written. Kilroy's theatre is a probing, unsettled, truly imagined place, transcending realism and naturalism, but well able to entertain and delight as much as shock. With the stakes that high, the voltage must be right. So he moves on.

In Bologna in the autumn of 2000 at a centenary conference on Wilde, a distinguished Italian academic and writer, responding to a general discussion on Kilroy's *The Secret Fall of Constance Wilde*, drew the audience's attention to his version of Pirandello's *Six Characters in search of an Author*. 'Kilroy is an Italian playwright; he is a European playwright. That's where he belongs'. I knew exactly what was meant. The audience knew what was meant: it is the fascinating, utterly unique and mysterious space, which Tom Kilroy inhabits.

iii

So there I was, sitting in a room in a forgotten part of the west of Ireland, a town battered around between pillar and post—a town, to all intents and purposes, no longer sure what to make of itself. Around me were in-laws, my wife, son and daughter. The talk was hectic, it being some time since we had visited my mother-in-law, her sister and her brother, all of whom were in their eighties. The gathering was in the small living room that looks out to a main road. The talk drifted unpredictably from one thing to another, with the past like a rudder, shifting us this way and that. Of Michael Collins and who had killed him; of England during 'the War', where my aunt had worked as a district nurse; of weaver-fish, whose reactive prongs can poison and numb an arm for months; of life in gaol during the War of Independence; of a returned distant relative and his family; of recent deaths and how they stripped the town of more of the old inhabitants—people who had experienced Ireland's history first-hand, participated in some of it but for the rest were outside and resigned, their feeling for history and politics determined by that place. I was sitting in the room listening and, after a while, I turned the radio on and heard someone discuss

'Poetry and Modern Society'. The difference was immediate.

With the room so full of talk —details of history, fragments of politics, of de Valera's head looking like that of an Indian's, of the weather and how it was changing—the sheer cacophonous energy was of many voices telling their own story and all seeking to be heard. And here on the radio was one voice, calm and controlled, being listened to, presumably with interest, in various homes, flats and rooms throughout the country.

The contrast is stark and severe but it does portray the kind of forces with which a poet must deal. Maybe not at the level of an individual poem, a specific image or scene, but in the backroom of the imagination, where poems are first made and developed, that clambering-for-expression, with its own vitality and insistence, exerts a special influence on what a poet writes.

This influence leads in 'two directions' at the same time—away from the gaggle and Babel's tower of living but also towards it, trying to hold those elements of it with which one can cope. Rarely is there a 'satisfactory' balance. The poet is confined to only a part of speech. A poet today, and possibly always, tries to make a poem that is entire and complete, unlike life where failure, defeat, injustice and pain so often interrupt and snatch freedom away. This is not to suggest that poets and poetry in the modern world must necessarily speak as if success, triumph, equality, hope and love were abandoned concepts. But I don't want to sound like an evangelist. Hope, love, injustice are just words, abstractions in the same way that the word 'language' is when related to the scene I've just described. I think too of another scene.

It is the late fifties in the sitting room of a red-bricked house in a terraced row of seven houses, wedged between Belfast's Cave Hill and the Lough: a world of small gardens, minute backyards; a dark scullery and two flights of creaking stairs that lead past the bathroom, like a look-out post. The mock stained-glass spangling light on the landing with two bedrooms, their fireplaces blocked, huge wardrobes and uncertain windows and at the top of the house, my own den, with its slanting ceilings, the piles of family mementoes and sheet music stashed in the corner and the chimney alive with sparrows.

In the front room, a large mirror leans above the mantelpiece before which a baize card-table is placed; to its right, a closed

Steinway piano, and to the left a bay window basking in the last of the late afternoon light. You can hear, just about, the tock of a grandfather clock on the landing. Also my grandmother's voice instructing a young girl from the district how to recite a poem 'properly'. It is Wednesday: elocution class.

Ethel, light-opera singer, shop assistant, belle, has in front of her *Palgrave's Treasury* opened at 'The Daffodils'. The girl, one of many, speaks the words with urgent feeling, the stresses and inflections in keeping with convention. The girl watches her own mouth in the mirror as Ethel mouths the syllables in a prompting mime.

For Ethel, it is a love and a profession. She taps out the rhythm like a conductor. The poem sings in a controlled and articulate manner. It has been mastered and the girl, in a pretty dress, will win a little cup and go into the world confident of the way she speaks, vowels like balloons, the head swaying ever so slightly from side to side. Until, probably, marriage, and the certain slow reclaiming of her own accent from that sophisticated gloss, which did not really help her 'get on' in the world after all.

This scene, which I witnessed as a small boy in my grandmother's house, opening doors to the hopeful and ambitious, comes to my mind when I think about the 'discipline' of the poetic craft. And here too, both scenes play across each other—the helter-skelter of impressions; the mannered poise; the fragments and figments of history; the cultivated grace; the 'nationalist' west; the 'unionist' north-east, each entailing its own hurt and insecurities, pride and prejudice, and how these are expressed differently. This is where the poet comes in, uncalled-for, but there all the same, summarising the complexity as best as he or she can, discerning what is humanly possible.

The greatest influence on a writer is the past and its relevance is pervasive. Often it is only when that past is unearthed that a poet begins to make sense of his or her own imaginings. Somehow the recovery of the world of the past not only helps a poet show what makes up the world but also helps make it a more 'liveable' place in the here and now. In this sense, a poet is strictly 'anti-nostalgic'.

In my own case, most of my poems are about this process. It is the voices of mood and the objective turn of events, which fascinate me, how they live in the memory, unsettling, probing, and making us think and feel in certain ways. And if memory is, as William Carlos Williams called it in his poem 'The Descent', "a kind of accomplishment/a sort of renewal/even/an initiation", so much the better.

One night in the mid-eighties, after giving a poetry reading in Gort, Co Galway, a town full of literary resonance, I watched a bunch of kids pump pinball machines in one of those anonymous hamburger joints. It was a cool damp evening without a cloud in the sky. The sound of a rock-band blared out the door. A police car patrolled down the square high above which stood a statue of Christ the King. Most of the other shops and houses of the main street were shut and dark. Behind them the countryside stretched away, crossed by a railway track, small farms and various clumps of forest, forgotten old houses and endless lanes leading somewhere. For some reason, that night made me think of how the time had flown since I arrived first, like any stranger, asking for directions.

Chronicles of Americana

Picture this. It's 1967, Belfast, in what would be called upper north side in the US. The neighbourhood is very 'mixed'. All forms of Protestantism—from the imposing Church of Ireland to sturdy Presbyterian and Methodist churches to evangelical halls of worship; Catholic, Jewish and (I dare say) private religions which we knew nothing about at the time. The streetscape is traditional urban: main thoroughfares which sweep down from the high rise of the Antrim hills into the city centre; overlooking the horseshoe of the Lough and the far side of east Belfast, now the industrial hub of Belfast since most of the mills of the west have closed or are closing. The houses range from villas set in their own wooded grounds and lawns to discrete avenues of fine double-fronted three or four storied red brick houses with small enough gardens out front but long strips of land out back, to more modest terraces built at the turn of the 19th into the 20th century, mirroring the larger houses, with stained glass windows on the landings, and yards instead of gardens. Behind them a network of 'between the wars' housing, decent, compact, with their own square of garden, backing on to uncultivated fields and the start of a new estate of about forty custom built homes for the newly prosperous working young couples in their twenties and early thirties. The rising generation, that is, married in the Sixties, with great expectations in mind of a good life.

In one of the older houses, in the front room that looks out on to a busy arterial road, which is one of the main links between the city centre and the flourishing suburban hinterland, two young lads are staring through the large fronted bay window, as cars and buses, vans and deliveries (laundry, bread, milk, coal, you name it), window cleaners, piano tuners, hedge cutters, painters and decorators, move up and down, passing men and women walking the avenue, going about their own every day business. The two lads are looking out the bay window while the room is utterly filled with the sound of Bob Dylan at full tilt.

No one is in the entire house but themselves. They may be smoking Sobraine cigarettes, or Olivier, or Nelson or, if things are a bit tight, the deadly Woodbine or Park Drive. They could be listening to any one of Dylan's albums from the early 1960s—*Freewheelin' Bob Dylan* was a favourite—or one of the more recent releases such as *Blonde on Blonde*, the mind-shifting sound of *John Wesley Harding* or *Nashville Skyline*.

In a couple of years time, by about 1971, it had all changed, more or less, as Belfast, and in particular, the 'mixed' district in which those two young men had grown up, was pitched into 'The Troubles' and the life of the avenues and streets, the terraces and lane ways, turned ever inwards.

For a substantial section of the WWII generation, growing up in the Sixties, Dylan was *the* transcendent voice, his lyrics and restless eye on contemporary life recorded the travails, expectations, anxieties and hopes about the big world of which, along with millions of others, those two lads felt themselves to be a curious questioning part.

'I was born in the spring in 1941', writes Dylan, 'the Second World War was already raging in Europe, and America would soon be in it. The world was being blown apart and chaos was already driving its fist into the face of all new visitors. If you were born around this time or, were living and alive, you could feel the old world go and the new one beginning'.

Even when many of the American terms of reference passed people by, Dylan's un-heroic, wry, urbane, sardonic intelligence sounded very familiar and the opening towards sensitivity (indeed sentiment) which his songs and music offered, remains 'forever young', forty or so years later. Reading the first volume of his marvellous *Chronicles*, a classic memoir, has the same impact. It describes a world that has gone and a 'lifestyle', commitment, and experience which is also, probably, no longer possible in the market-driven, niche-determined, global village of Anglo-American popular culture.

Chronicles is, quite simply, a book that reaches far beyond the (albeit) vast base of Dylan fans. It stands on its own literary merits as a fascinating imaginative portrait of America, its ethnically diverse neighbourhoods of naturalised emigrants (such as Dylan's own grandparents), its hopes and assumptions, turned upside down by the (there is no other word for it) obsessional fascination of a young boy with folk music and the journey which took him from Hibbing, Minnesota via the Village, Manhattan, on an never-ending tour, performing and recording his own songs and music before the world stage.

It was, and is, an obsession with folk music that straddles all kinds of music—from black, 'roots' or 'race' music, as it was once called, to country music and all the way through to political ballads and the traditional. As he recounts in *Chronicles* Dylan learnt it all—and I do mean 'all'. His story is literally crammed with songs.

At times when he moves into the theosophy of guitar playing and song structures ('a highly controlled system of playing' which the reader can discover for his or her self on page 157), there is the strongest hint of self-parody. But the re-creation of city life in fifties and sixties New York, the sheer poetic intensity with which he recaptures his own experiences of that world as an outsider, is second to none. This is writing of the highest order indeed and one can only nod at the surprise expressed by various 'literary' figures that Dylan could actually produce such a work.

There is, too, at the very centre of *Chronicles* a tragic note, a sense of the madness of the political world and a rage that, contradictory as it sounds, took Dylan away from the familiar and habitual world of his upbringing into the fickle intensity of the world's media and the mess that we know as 'celebrity'.

If Dylan were a poet or novelist he would have been a Nobel laureate by now. When you read *Chronicles* just keep in the back of your mind any one of the hundreds of great songs which he has written. For me, for starters, it's 'Bob Dylan's Dream' which I still hear as if for the first time, and the staggering, peer-less, 'Masters of War'. Dylan is truly unique; the story he has told in *Chronicles* universal. As Sean O Hagan, remarked in the *Observer*, 'even in his seventh decade, Dylan is the great enigmatic genius of our time; beyond pop, beyond rock, beyond any label you dare pin on him'.

Alas, the same cannot be said for one of Dylan's early influences, Jack Kerouac. For his life, like his writing, is a story of two photographs. On the cover of Paul Maher's methodical biography *Kerouac: The Definitive Biography* (2004) Jack Kerouac is the All-American star footballer, one time marine and merchant seaman, of brash good looks, slicked back hair, the Windsor knotted tie loosened around the poplin-shirted neck, staring the camera down, over his left shoulder, like a *film noir* moon, the light blurs in what might be a hotel room. Kerouac takes up the full picture, confident, self-propelling, no messing. The second photograph, taken the year before his death in 1969 at age 47, reveals a totally different figure, slumped in a chair, bloated with drink, the shadow of good looks blunted by the shocking body language of an invalid, his arm around his friend, John Sampas—a life that burned brightly but burned out, well before its time.

Author of one of the great post WW2 novels, *On the Road* (1957), Kerouac pioneered a form of 'spontaneous prose' (which it wasn't) and trans-genre writing—an ebullient, lyrical, physical mix of autobiography as fiction (which it was). He was the centre of a group of writers in America who fought for artistic freedom in the aftermath of WW2 and the conformist Fifties. The 'Beats', as they were to be known worldwide, consisted of lost souls—dangerous, broken and damaged in many ways, among them criminals, junkies and 'high class' girls, looking for thrills. They all shared a restlessness and curiosity about the American continent and spent most of their lives trying to find out what and where America 'was'; not the American dream, so much, as the American dawn. Their lives makes 'Sex and the City' look like a ride in the park.

Both Allen Ginsberg, who Kerouac met in New York, and Neal Cassady, were like Kerouac, from immigrant backgrounds; William Seward Burroughs, another key figure, was however a Harvard graduate, grandson of the inventor of the Burroughs adding machine, and lived off two hundred dollars a month (a tidy sum) provided by his wealthy and long-suffering parents.

The vulnerabilities of Kerouac's upbringing in a French-speaking Canadian family, the loss of his elder brother, Gerard, at a young age; the early death of his father, and the unhealthy obsessions of his mother with whom he was to live for the best part of his life—were matched in Cassady's shattered childhood of sleeping in dosshouses with his alcoholic father. Ginsberg saw his own mother crack at a relatively early age and to live her last years in a state hospital.

The heady ether that drew these men together—drugs, booze, sexual experiment, sentimentality and living on a knife-edge—scandalized the proprieties of mainstream America while, simultaneously, fascinating the burgeoning print and television media.

With the success of *On the Road* Kerouac was swept on a tide of admirers and imitators as the celebrity of 'The Beats' brought undoubted fame and recognition, particularly to the unholy alliance of the foursome, which he had immortalized in the novel. They pursued their hallucinogenic 'new vision', primed with Benzedrine and booze, with readings of Rimbaud, Dostoevsky, Joyce, Thomas Wolfe, Dylan Thomas, the anarchistic influence of Californian Kenneth Rexroth (still a poet worth looking for) and what Ginsberg called their 'secret heroes', particularly jazz musicians like Charlie Parker and Dizzie Gillespie. The 'risk' of jazz, solo performances of searing emotional intensity, was the sound and structure Kerouac admired and attempted to reproduce along with the speech rhythms and phrasing of American English—so different from his native French-Canadian tongue. Indeed the rigid, Jansenist catholic pieties of his upbringing clashed continuously throughout his life, as the freedoms he sought were held in check with guilt and paranoia and strangeness set in. His biographer informs us that Kerouac 'kept a lifelong list of every woman he had sex with, along with the type and frequency', though not it, seems, with the men.

In this extensive biography the gory details of Kerouac's life stack up in front of the uninitiated reader and obscure even further the writing upon which he expended such mind-altering energy. Little time is spent on the many books he wrote, and their reception is left largely unaccounted for and under-analyzed.

Caught in the headlights of his own celebrity, even in his final retreat, mulling over the lack of critical respect, rejecting the detractors, Kerouac's destructive spiral veered between aggressive, mocking narcissistic self-belief (check out his priceless *Paris Review* with Ted Berrigan) and the intoxicating, lethal frailties that unmanned him. If the world does not make writers like Kerouac any more, only pale pretenders, dashing off to Rehab before the next confessionalist interview takes hold, it's probably because, like many other forms of popular culture, writing is now part of the very media and entertainment business which Kerouac saw coming but could not outpace or handle. The wretched diet of colloquial racism and anti-Semitism of his upbringing, inflamed by the rhetoric of Macarthyite Fifties, meant that Kerouac's politics were always going to be volatile and incoherent. No wonder he kept wind side of the Hippy Sixties with their veneer of radical politics.

The tragedy is that no one seemed to mind (except boyhood pals and his old girlfriend whom he eventually married) but instead entertained his eventual fall. When that came, as Paul Maher has it, Kerouac's body rejected 'the donated blood' before 'he lapsed into unconsciousness' where he lay 'for fifteen painful hours before being declared dead'. He had literally killed himself with drink. Fifty years after its composition, the original 1951 version of *On the Road* 'set a world record for the highest paid bid for a literary manuscript at auction', bought for $2.43 million by the owner of the NFL's Indianapolis Colts.

Kerouac's Proustian plan, a series of interlinked novels, building into one great saga, was never completed. A ghost project, perhaps even a delusion, it haunted his imagination to the bitter end. For Kerouac, freedom had existed by proving himself a difficult, moving target; when he slowed down the writing seems to have done the same. Not interested in his daughter, Jan, he had used up his friends until there were precious few capable of bearing the late night drunken rants on long distance calls. Burroughs and Ginsberg outlived him by twenty years; Cassady, high on speed, Seconal and pulque, a potent Mexican drink, was found 'comatose' by the train-tracks to San Miguel, his unclaimed body cremated and the ashes sent to his estranged wife.

Ill at ease outside America, suspicious even of those friends drawn to his obviously infectious personality, Kerouac was possibly happiest in the company of strangers—those whom he picked up on the road, in bars, diners, gas stations, on Greyhound buses; on the move, like himself, through the awe-inspiring magnificence of the American landscape; temporary, transit families of his own making, providing uncomplicated, un-lasting emotional ties from which he could draw some fictional life before fleeing again like a fugitive; running away, it looks like, from himself. Or maybe the expectations he had of himself as a writer. One way or another, American writers, novelists particularly, live a doubled edge reality, both costlier and with greater reward, than most European writers. For poets, the situation is less clear, certainly if one takes to heart the witness of Saul Bellow.

'The country is proud of its dead poets', proclaims Charlie Citrine in Bellow's brilliant novel, *Humboldt's Gift*, 'It takes terrific satisfaction in the poet's testimony that the USA is too tough, too big, too much, too rugged, that American reality is overpowering. And to be a poet is a school thing, a skirt thing, a church thing'. In the *Oxford Book of American Poetry* (2006), chosen and edited by David Lehman with the assistance of associate editor, John Brehn—a magnificent feat of book-publishing, let it be said—poetry strikes back. To balance the 'overpowering' American reality, these one thousand pages and more, act as an impressive counterblast, if ever there was one. For whatever about the travails in the politics of contemporary American governance, take time out and revel instead in the bounty of American poetry. Such a grand narrative it is too.

The story, according to Lehman and Brehn, begins appropriately enough with uncertainty, in Anne Bradstreet (c.1612-1672), 'To sing of Wars, of Captaines, and of Kings,/Of Cities founded, Common-Wealths begun', and concludes with the Massachusetts-born son of Chinese parents, poet and art-critic, John Yau (b.1950). That is roughly three and a half centuries worth of poetry.

The swings and roundabouts of critical fashion have levelled out around many of the international names as we move into the 19th century with Ralph Waldo Emerson (1803-1882), one in a fascinatingly comprehensive and lasting line of poet-essayists who hail from New England. The head-note on Emerson makes the point that he 'seems sometimes to have invented, or at least envisioned, American literature as an entity unto itself rather than as a tributary of a mainstream English or British tradition'.

The tributary turned into a flood by the mid-century in the persona of Walt Whitman (1819-1892) with his magisterially influential 'Song of Myself' (included in full in the anthology), along with the troubled immanence of Herman Melville (1819-1891)

and the haunted figure of Edgar Allan Poe (1809-1849)—of whom
Richard Wilbur remarked, 'it is Poe who most challenges the reader
not only to read him but to solve him', a phrase that could well
turn the key on much American poetry of the following mid-20th
century. And of course there is Miss Emily Dickinson (1830-
1886), born in Amherst, Mass., spending 'nearly all her life within
its confines', and imagining a life without:

> Wild nights!—Wild nights!
> Were I with thee
> Wild Nights should be
> Our luxury!
>
> Futile—the Winds -
> To a Heart in port -
> Done with the Compass -
> Done with the Chart!
>
> Rowing in Eden -
> Ah! The Sea!
> Might I but moor—Tonight -
> In Thee.

One of the real achievements of this anthology is that we can read
the great poets in the context of lesser known, but richly rewarding
figures, so that by the time we reach the first great twentieth
century American poet, Robert Frost (1874-1963), there is a sense
of historical momentum and psychological force breaking into
many different directions, from which point on, the roll call is
utterly mind-blowing: Frost, Stein, Stevens, Carlos Williams,
Pound, Moore—*ah, Marianne*—Eliot, e e cummings, Hart Crane,
Allen Tate, and—surprisingly, Auden. At which we pause. *Auden?*
The quintessential European poet became a U.S. citizen, but
according to the editor, Auden 'belongs [in the anthology] not only
because of the poems he wrote in and sometimes about places like
New York City...but because of his importance to a whole generation
of American poets'. This is daft. A similar case could be made for
Lorca. But the glitch shouldn't take away from the sheer power and
weight of the American poets in this splendid book. The significance
of their lives, too, is revealed in succinct notes, quirkily telling the

reader the causes of death in many individual cases, and also pointing out just how many of the leading poets of the last century—some, alas, such as Anthony Hecht passing away quite recently,—were themselves soldiers in bloody wars from WW2 to Korea and Vietnam. Or like Robert Lowell, Kenneth Rexroth and William Stafford were conscientious objectors. But the range is here to judge for yourself: somewhat marginalised figures, for example, George Oppen and Charles Bukowski sit alongside the once revered Edna St Vincent Millay; Bessie Smith is here and so is Dylan, the exceptional Sylvia Plath and the excellent James Tate, the obsessive James Wright and the life-loving and tragically short-lived, Frank O Hara. And dear Elizabeth Bishop, the belle of the ball, with Theodore Roethke by her side. It can't get much better than that now, can it?

I should have had a copy of the anthology as diversion on my way through Shannon Airport en route to the States. I saw a woman hold a handwritten note against the double-glazed window of the transit lounge which read, GOD BLESS YOU. GOD BLESS AMERICA. The young black soldier, who looked about fourteen, passed by without noticing. It was unquestionably his first time outside his home county and he looked scared stiff. He could well be one of the faces which appear one day on PBS in silent homage to those killed in Iraq.

Iraq is everywhere in America: on the television, from the manikin-like 'anchor' broadcasters who swap sound-bites to brawling Fox News to heavy-weight media sessions at which Administration press officers, like senior school prefects, do the president's bidding, to the latest revelation of wrongdoing. And yet, notwithstanding this avalanche of coverage, little real light is shed by the interminable number of 'experts'(on terrorism, on the 'Middle East') who are promoting their books, think-tanks, or Institutes. It really is a tower of Babel, but if you have God on your side, well, the likes of this kind of malarkey fits all sizes:

> We're an empire now, and when we act, we create our own reality. And while you're studying that reality- judiciously, as you will—we'll act again, creating other new realities, which you can study too, and that's how things will sort out.

This 'Bush-speak', from an aide quoted by Ron Suskind in October 2004 is part of the dream world unpicked by Seattle-based British novelist, critic and travel writer, Jonathan Raban in his excellent series of dispatches from the American home front *My Holy War* (2006). Several years on, the bravado has shrunk to one of those brittle smiles on 'Meet the Press', but *My Holy War* is not an 'I told you so', self-regarding book. It is full of Raban's knowledgeable fascination with America, its mighty embracing culture, its literature and its people. (Raban was one of the first to introduce the great American poet, Robert Lowell to this side of the Atlantic). But the curiosity about Bush and his (disappearing) troupe of ideologues is infectious:

> It's as if America, since September 11, has been reconstituted as a colonial New England village: walled in behind a stockade to keep out Indians (who were seen as in thrall to the devil); centred on its meeting house in whose elevated pulpit stands Bush, the plain-spun preacher, a figure of nearly totalitarian authority in the community of saints. The brave young men of the village are out in the wilderness, doing the Lord's work, fighting wicked spirits who would otherwise be inside the stockade burning down Main Street and the meetinghouse. That, at least, is how the presidential handlers have tried to paint things.

Raban is also good on the causes of all the paranoia and fear. He tracks the ideology of fundamentalism in the September 11 hijackers, and those who have fallen in their footsteps, with almost chilly clarity, quoting from sources such as Sayyid Qutb's *Milestones* (1964), 'the primary inspirational book of the jihad movement'. When it comes to recognizing the context out of which the bombers emerged in Europe and Britain, Raban's description is worth quoting in full. The September 11 hijackers, he writes, 'learned their brand of murderous revolutionism not in the Middle East, where they grew up, but in the west, where they were students.

> In particular, they congregated in the polyglot suburb of Harburg, south of the river Hamburg; a place that in its social and economic make-up looks a lot like the shabbier bits of Leeds, Yorkshire, or the London suburbs of Stockwell,

Tulse Hill, and Streatham Hill, where the London bombers found their lodgings—that unpicturesque terrain of flats, terraced housing, betting shops, malodorous hairdressers, ethnic groceries and restaurants, stalled traffic, broken pavements, boarded-up shop fronts, the amiable muddle of gimcrack domestic and commercial architecture dating from the 1880s to the near present. Nowhere could be more 'western' in its style of down-at-heel free enterprise. This is the landscape of lax secular capitalism, out of which people—many of them recent immigrants—have quarried their own small communities, where indigent loners can easily find a room to let, the natural habitat of the eccentric sect or coterie. Anything goes.

Jonathan Raban knows what he is talking about here; he also knows a thing or two about the Middle East. If you want a book that tries to understand the bloody mess we're in, *My Holy War* is the one.

Enduring myths

i

Of the war poets whom W B Yeats *did* include in his notorious *Oxford Book of Modern Verse* (1936) Siegfried Sassoon's 'On Passing the New Menin Gate' looks upon the commemorative monument to The Great War dead with savage indignation:

> And here with pride
> 'Their name liveth forever', the Gateway claims.
> Was ever an immolation so belied
> As these intolerably nameless names?
> Well might the Dead who struggled in the slime
> Rise and deride this sepulcher of crime.

Sassoon's life (1886-1967) was 'forever' haunted by those war experiences which, according to Max Egremont's authorized biography, *Siegfried Sassoon: A Biography* (2005), 'were restricted to inauspicious times, to the prelude and start of the Somme in 1916, to the Hindeberg trenches in April 1917 at the time of the battle of Arras, just before the failure of the Nivelle offensive; then to the early summer of 1918 when the Allies were still reeling from the massive German attacks of March. Back in Britain, he heard of an apparently bloody, bad end to the Somme'. Twice wounded, decorated with the Military Cross for valour and bravery, Sassoon's survival—unlike other war poets with whom his name is bound, such as Wilfred Owen and Isaac Rosenberg—is told in all its anxious, yearning self-obsession in Egremont's somewhat bloated book of almost 600 pages. Like all master narratives the elusive truth to Sassoon's life lies elsewhere.

Sassoon's Jewishness, his homosexuality and in his conflicted desire to be part of the aristocratic 'in crowd', brings to mind Oscar Wilde's rapid life and perilous times—a connection underscored by Sassoon's friendship with Robert Ross. But this story resides (again a little like Wilde's) tacitly inscribed in Sassoon's best-selling poetry and prose writing: *Memoirs of a Fox-Hunting Man*, *Memoirs of an Infantry Officer* and *Sherton's Progress*. While the first volume of the Memoirs was being lauded for the 'ease and quiet and lovely Englishness' and Sassoon being compared to Shakespeare, he saw *Fox-Hunting Man* as, in Egremont's words, 'a sham, denying the most important parts of him'; 'almost none of the things I would like to write', is how Sassoon described the book. What was 'left out' was an extraordinary life of great luxury, generosity, emotional turbulence, masochism, Puritanism, repression, denial and never-ending self dramatization. In the latter cause Sassoon was ably assisted by a string of lovers, hangers-on, cheerleaders, patrons, groupies, and partygoers and, ultimately, those who really cared. Egremont's biography is in fact a portrait gallery of a caste of English eccentrics at a point of terminable decline, post WW1 and pre WW2. Thomas Hardy at Max Gate is ' a shrine' but his passing in 1928 reveals Sassoon as a weathervane, spinning this way and that, continually lavishing gifts of money and presents upon his many friends, including the Sitwells, and upon those who had been (and might become again) friends, such as Robert Graves. With so much temperature taking of feeling and the swift judging of others, (behind backs, in the diaries of the time) it's sometime hard to keep up with who is in and who is out. These folks were certainly well tuned to the expanding world of celebrity and publicity. Yet Sassoon's life story moves from the sexual obsessions which, according to his biographer, 'plagued him', to marriage, the birth of his adored son, George, and a parable life lived in relative isolation as an English country gentleman who had converted to Catholicism.

The to-ings and fro-ings of his gay life with Stephen Tennant are the stuff of a Wildean drama. Stephen who insisted upon travelling with his valet, Nanny and beloved parrot, lived until 1986, his last years 'a recluse at Wilsford, his bed strewn with seashells, sheaves of his own drawings, and the manuscript of *Lascar* [his novel]; fat with turbulent orange hair, still proud of what he thought of as his shapely legs'. Egremont is unrelenting in reminding the reader of Sassoon's sexual desires, from boy soldiers to actors to princes (including one related to the Kaiser) but less sure of his ground when it comes to Sassoon's fascinating ethnic and religious background, elided by the need to keep analysis (and historical and cultural background) to a minimum as the welter of daily pedantic detail piles up.

'Kentish' is how Edmund Blunden described Sassoon's writing, 'healthy and pastoral' glosses Egremont. But if the biographer's opening description of Sassoon as 'an uncertain Englishman' sound almost tragic, indeed in some sense, farcical, the concluding last words of this important study sound a tad chauvinistic: 'Sassoon evokes a lost, decent England achieved only in the imagination, perhaps only in the imagination of those a little outside this country of the heart. The myth is strong, even mesmeric, better and more honourable than most myths by which nations live, and [Sassoon's] writings have helped it to endure'. Or not as the case may be.

Here is a scene Sassoon recounts in his fictionalised autobiography:

> This morning. Suez Canal from train. Garden at Ismalia—
> a bit of blossom and greenery among sandy wastes.
> Waiting at Canal bridge for two big ships to go by. Talked
> to two Irish officers in the train. One knew Ledwidge the
> poet, and said, "He could imitate birds and call them to
> him"—a tiny glimpse of "real life" in this desert of officer
> mentality. Am feeling ill and keep on coughing.

Sassoon had earlier that year, 1918, left Limerick where he had been stationed for a brief spell—post shell-shock, and post his controversial rejection of the Great War—and where he had also written some of his finest poems. Little wonder, as he falls into conversation with two fellow (Irish) officers entrain to Egypt that Francis Ledwidge's name should gladly come up in conversation. Ledwidge also appears in the *War Letters* of that extraordinarily tragic poet and composer Ivor (Bertie) Gurney—who had spent the last fifteen years of his relatively brief life in a mental hospital having suffered a calamitous breakdown just before the end of WW1, in which he saw front line action, was wounded and gassed at Passchendaele. It's August 1917: 'And so Ledwidge is dead…He was a true poet, and the story of his life is (now) a sad but romantic tale, like that of so many others, so wastefully spent. Yet the fire may not have struck in them save for the war; anyway it was to be, and is'.

Francis Ledwidge, who was already making a name for himself in Ireland prior to his death in WW1, makes no appearance in the monumental and magnificent *Handbook of British & Irish War Poetry* (2007), edited by Professor of English literature at Exeter University, Tim Kendall. Throughout the 37 essays, amounting to a whopping 750 pages, there is curiously little critical recognition—despite the title—of Irish poets from the south of Ireland and who fought, along with many thousands of their compatriots, in either or both world wars. Recent research has shown the numbers of men and women involved were substantial, even if, for far too long, their wartime experience was barely acknowledged in official circles. Times have changed and critical and public awareness is certainly more advanced on this issue today.

Scattered reference here and there to Easter 1916 signatories, to Patrick McGill, Charles Donnelly (who died in 1937 fighting during the Battle of Jarama in the Spanish Civil War) but the real focus when Ireland comes into view is with the post WW2 generation of northern poets, including Michael Longley, Seamus Heaney, and somewhat surprisingly, Paul Muldoon. Yet nothing on Frank Ormsby's groundbreaking collection *A Northern Spring* (1986), which dramatised the experience of American soldiers in Northern Ireland on the cusp of 'D' Day landings, an audacious and powerful album of thirty six poems that would have fitted perfectly into such a handbook as this:

> A litter of blanks, a rubble of rusted cans,
> our curved huts in farmyards filled with hens,
> the whorl of an air-raid shelter through a bank
> of ferns and briars.
> In a wood that is not home there is no pain
> to think how we'll be forgotten.

('36: Postscripts')

Equally perplexing, given the fascinating work covered by the *Handbook*, as contributors range through the different cultural and historical perspectives of Scottish, English and Welsh poets and their literary contexts, that Thomas MacGreevy, WW1 veteran, Irish nationalist, and conduit for the European modernist writers such as his close friends, James Joyce and Samuel Beckett, makes no showing, even though his poetry is clearly shot through with his responses to the loss of fellow soldiers, as well as his visualization of the strange lethal unreality of the everyday world at war.

In his timely update on the present situation, David Wheatley's 'Contemporary War and the Non-Combatant Poet', reports:

> The true element of the war poem is the shortfall between artistic and actual justice, the justice it does to its own material and the human justice it cannot deliver, a gap the writer can choose to explore with full artistic honesty or evade through self-deception and wish-fulfilment.

Given our own time's appalling signature of 'shock and awe', *The Handbook* is required reading and should be in every school, college and community library the length and breadth of the country. It is a lasting memoir of how ghastly war is and how redemptive poetry can be as a way of offering respite from the seeming endlessness of life 'so wastefully spent'. 'Someday', wrote Ivor Gurney, 'all this experience may be crystallized and glorified in me; and men shall learn what thoughts haunted the minds of men who watched the darkness grimly in desolate places'.

When I was a young boy in Belfast in the fifties one of my grandmother's friends who used to attend little soirees in our front room with his wife, Ella, was called 'Uncle' Oswald. He was a small plump man who looked like a seal. Along with many others who attended those gatherings he accompanied on the piano ('vamping' it was called) as my grandmother sang or recited. Uncle Oswald had been 'gassed' during the war and was 'invalided out', I heard. Phrases that made little sense then, and even in church on memorial days, sitting under paper thin colour flags of some imperial army battalion, the reality of what he and those other war veterans had gone through—men in regimental blazers hirpling along to the Royal Legion Hall, parading on Remembrance Sunday, in their berets on July 1st commemorations—remained hidden behind the wall of the (then) more recent WWII with its iconography of black out blinds, ration books, Blitzed landscape and televised history. These WW1 survivors are now all but gone, save perhaps for a handful in France or Germany. Their history logged in battalion records, diaries and in cenotaphs, on the fields of crosses in Flanders, in family archives of photographs, ribbons, medals, keepsakes and mementoes of what was known as The Great War.

In the English-speaking world, the reality of their experience was caught for all time in the poetry of a generation first exposed to the horror of trench warfare. The war poetry of an officer class, including Siegfried Sassoon, Robert Graves, Wilfred Owen, with soldier poets such as Edward Thomas, Ivor Gurney and Francis Ledwidge, made it impossible for any subsequent political and/or military revisions to take over what it had really been like to fight a technological world war of poison gas and mass land and air bombardment. The human cost in terms of physical and mental damage is quite simply mind-numbing and the poetic witness inscribed this reality in western consciousness to respect, or ignore at our peril.

In her fastidious biography, *Isaac Rosenberg: The Making of a Great War Poet, A New Life* (2008) Jean Moorcroft Wilson, author of biographies of Sassoon and Charles Hamilton Sorley, has rendered the prewar life and war time death of an extraordinary talent. Both as painter and poet, Rosenberg was exceptional, surviving the immensely difficult years as a young Jewish boy, from a poor emigrant family at the turn of the nineteenth century, first in Bristol, and then in the East End of London. The slightly frosty narrative never fails to shock with just how rough times were and just how hard people had to fight for a decent standard of living, working all hours to attain both. Without patronage (in both senses of the word, 'condescending praise' is how Wilson describes Ezra Pound's 'help') education was not available, or at best, hard come by.

The young group of artistically multi-talented Jewish boys and girls met in public libraries, formed ad hoc support groups, sought out help wherever they could, and many, Rosenberg included, started to (very) slowly make a name for themselves as visual artists and writers in a host society marred with prejudice. Born in 1890, Rosenberg's recognition would only really come posthumously after a relatively brief life which saw him killed in the horrendous March offensive at the Western Front on April 1st 1918.

The life as told in Jean Moorcroft Wilson's biography, including Rosenberg's stay in South Africa, and journey into the war, reveals systemic anti-Semitism in both civilian and military walks of life. But what emerges from her research is a powerful portrait of both man and times: 'His reasons for enlisting', Wilson tells us, 'unlike visions of valour, patriotism and sacrifice which motivated poets such as Brooke and, initially, Sassoon, were economically driven... It was simply because he could not get work and needed to earn some money to send home to his struggling mother'.

While the harmonic of his poetry was heavily influenced by his Yiddish speaking parents, 'the shyness, embarrassment and social ineptness of his unprepossessing figure' was, according to Wilson, 'balanced by a total dedication to art which turned him at times into the mysterious Romantic figure of his self portraits and those painted of him by others'.

In a letter written in the month before he died, Rosenberg revealed just how much death was playing on his mind, a presentiment that understandably worked its way into many a soldier's thoughts: 'We will become like mummies—look warm and lifelike, but a touch and we crumble to pieces'.

Driven back three weeks later, 'Rosenberg and his fellow soldiers in the 1st King's Own were ordered to "Stand-To"– in full equipment, prepared for battle'. He wrote his last poem, 'Through These Pale Cold Days' and sent it on March 28th to Marsh, his patron.

'At 3 a.m.', his biographer sums up, 'the Germans renewed their attack with an advance so rapid that Rosenberg found himself in the new front line'. While ordered to retreat he may well have 'volunteered for extra duty at the last moment'. He never reached the reserves, but was 'killed by a German raiding party at dawn ... his remains unrecovered in no-man's-land for almost a fortnight'. Found among the belongings of this wondrous human being was the following note:

> How small a thing is art. A little pain; disappointment, and any man feels a depth – a boundlessness of emotion, inarticulate thoughts no poet has ever succeeded in imag[in]ing. Death does not conquer me, I conquer death, I am the master.

ii

If WW1 haunted the imagination of English poets such as Rosenberg and Gurney, to the point of destroying their lives, England, or more accurately, versions of England have been a driving force in much of that country's greatest writing. Think of D H Lawrence.

Here he is in a letter, written in 1912, from his retreat in Villa Igea by Lake Garda in Italy. Lawrence is writing to one of his closest friends, Arthur William Mc Leod, and railing against the country he both loved and hated:

> I hate England and its hopelessness...I want to wash again, wash off England, the oldness and grubbiness and despair.

And in a reverie of his Italian hideaway, he rallies,

> Yesterday F. [Frieda, his partner] and I went down along the lake towards Maderno. We climbed down from a little olive wood, and swam. It was evening, so weird, and a great black cloud trailing across the lake. And tiny little lights of villages came out, so low down, right across the water. Then great lightnings spilt out. – No, I don't believe England need be so grubby.

It's the kind of contradictory intensity we normally associate with Irish writers such as Joyce or Beckett, when troubled thoughts of country clouded their minds. Lawrence's exilic wanderings throughout Europe, Australia, Mexico and elsewhere almost inevitably brought his imagination back to England, and the various places in which he had grown up, crucially, as a young boy in Nottinghamshire and thence into the troubled, compassionate and estranged writer of London and Cornwall.

There is indeed a curious history to later 20th century English writers' attitudes to their own English places: Philip Larkin's Coventry, is well known, but there is the etherealized English landscape of the much less publicly recognised poet, David Gascoyne, or Basil Bunting's re-imagining of his Northumbria boyhood in *Briggflatts* while the wonderful Thom Gunn, more appropriately associated with San Francisco, also wrote of Hampstead as if he were Patrick Kavanagh addressing Inniskeen.

Leeds, one of the great cities of industrial England, has produced its laureate in Tony Harrison as the class history of imperial Britain is refracted through the imaginative injunctions of this poet of passionate intelligence. Harrison is England, a version of its history, submerged now forever, under the welter of post-industrial, 'corporatised' reality. Harrison's poetry, in rejecting this 'new world' is not all, but much, of a radical nostalgia, not unlike Lawrence's visionary precedence.

Now collected in two substantial volumes—*Collected Poems* and *Collected Film Poetry* (both 2007)—Harrison's poetry reveals the turbulent sense of economic and cultural change as the city of his childhood and youth, and one of the cockpits of British industrial might, is charted from the pre-WW2 world of homogeneous family and domestic life, through community experience—of work, religion, history, language, social customs and expectations—into a difficult and painful re-imagining of all these things, in the multicultural world of contemporary England that took root in the late Sixties and early Seventies. Roughly at the same time the industrial cornerstones of the traditional English working class were collapsing. From the post-WW2 era, the familiar path of educational transition into university brought a new generation of writers to the fore, a new generation that cast doubt and uncertainty on the establishment mores and assumptions of English cultural and economic traditions. They looked in two directions simultaneously—along the fault-lines of working class life experiencing the pressures of economic downturn, and outwards to the wider, previously unimaginable cultural possibilities that educational opportunity had made possible. Harrison's imaginative dialectic swings like a Geiger counter between these energies and desires, artistic options and historical realities.

Tony Harrison's *Collected Poems* is, like no other, the most consistent poetic testimony to the politics of these structural changes in English 'national' self-consciousness. Finding the language in which to record this history, Harrison's often blunt and brutal obsessions (that on occasion teeter towards doggerel) are masked, like Samuel Johnson's, in the lithe forms of English and classical literary traditions and forms. Underpinning the lacerating dramatic exchanges between poet and skinhead in the era-defining poem of

Thatcher's years, 'V.', seen from the viewpoint of those less deceived, there runs one of the best-known idylls of English poetry, the much loved, much learned, 'Elegy Written in a Country Church Yard' by Thomas Gray:

> Jobless though they are, how can these kids,
> Even though their team's lost one more game,
> Believe that the 'Pakis', 'Niggers', even 'Yids'
> Sprayed on the tombstones here should bear the blame?

And throughout both *Collected Poems* and the challenging volume of *Collected Film Poetry*, which includes a fascinating self-study by Harrison in 'Flicks and This Fleeting Life', a portrait emerges of a public poet, enraged by the politics of his time, and making poetry out of this passion. It is not only England that features here, but the imperial afterlives of once foreign places—Nigeria, South America—, the respite of love and friendship and the shocking rebirth of war in 'A Cold Coming', set in the last Iraqi disaster. Whether writing for the stage in New York or the television in Britain, Harrison's vigorous, vocal English comes unquestionably from the living room fireside of his Leeds upbringing, an unmistakably dramatic voice which thankfully cannot 'pipe down'.

What place poetry really enjoys in our post-industrial world, how adequate the poet's voice is to the tasks of an increasingly marketed and celebrity-preoccupied culture such as that of the Anglophone world is, or maybe *was*, a burning critical issue. As Derek Mahon has it is his poem, 'Remembering the '90s':

> In the known future
> New books will be rarities in techno-culture,
> A forest of intertextuality like this,
> Each one a rare book and what few we have
> Written for prize-money and not for love,
> While the real books like vintage wines survive
> Among the antiquities.

If this *is* what the future holds so be it. As for the past, poet and scholar, Geoffrey Hill, in his monumental volume, *Collected Critical Writings* (2008), takes the reader on a soaring trip through the greats of English and classical literature, with the foundation stones of

European religious and literary culture formidably present throughout. Shakespeare, Ben Jonson, Jonathan Swift, Robert Southwell, rub shoulders with George Eliot, Hopkins, Coleridge, the watchful figure of Eliot is never too far away, alongside the American Kenyon Critics (Allen Tate, Cleanth Brooks, Matthhiessen), the WWI poets, such as Ivor Gurney, Charles Sorley and Isaac Rosenberg. All assemble in the brilliant dance of Hill's imaginative invention of an England and Englishness that seems, a little like the recurring biblical quotations and references, almost foreign to contemporary time and critical fashion.

For in many ways what strikes the reader most about this fascinating portrait of the intellectual life and concerns of one of England's leading poets is the sheer weight of Hill's commitment to the life of the imagination and the meaning of literary art. Time after time, he returns the focus of his critical attention to the foibles of the present, and in often quite unexpected ways, links the achievement of, say, Robert Southwell with the creative mind of Antonin Artaud.

Iris Murdoch's brilliant introduction to Jean-Paul Sartre sets up Hill's reading of several poets and philosophers and their ability to 'redeem the time', as Gerard Manley Hopkins's poetry emerges as 'dogged resistance'. Decadence is the enemy and what makes *Collected Critical Writings* such a surprise is that, even though the writing can become arch and obsessive in parts—there are several passages which simply enter Alice in Wonderland-like mazes of quotation and the reader is left wondering what all the fuss is over – the moral dignity and scholarly authority which Hill brings to his subjects is quite simply breath-taking at times, particularly when he is at his most direct, and allows his own English language to do the work for him.

The 'perspective requires', he remarks about the poetry of Andrew Marvell and Ben Jonson, 'utterance of deliberate cliché, but cliché rinsed and restored to function as responsible speech'. The moral weight is all in that word 'rinsed' which carries inside itself a vernacular history too. And it's this which fascinates about Hill's critical writing, for throughout there are the ghosts of previous English worlds, and words, and the integrity of the language, and history, out of which the great writers which he focuses upon have come since the beginning of an *English* literature is the bedrock of his accumulated study. Hill is adamant about 'literary in the best sense of the term', of 'products of the creative imaginative' and of how these fit into a moral and civic order within which people, ordinary people respond as readers, as citizens, as writers. *Collected Critical Writings* is all about such fundamental matters alongside the ins and outs of individual inflections in this poet or that dramatic scene.

The key to this study is in that all defining moment in the history of England (and of course, Europe)—the Great War. In the midst of the carnage the poetic voice held sway on subsequent generations and never has allowed the political and/or military experience to obscure what happened. In his critical tribute to Isaac Rosenberg, the young London Jewish émigré poet and painter, Hill has fashioned a portrait of our times as much as of one hundred years ago. It is a magnificent piece of writing that marries an historical understanding with humane sensitivity and critical judgment.

'In consideration of British and American poetry in the second half of the twentieth century,' Hill writes,

> the quotidian has been, with significant exceptions, over-valued as the authenticating factor in the work of the imagination. The poem itself, assessed in this way, becomes the author's promise to pay on demand, to provide real and substantial evidence of a suffering life for which the poem itself is merely a kind of tictac or flyer.

No more than in his poetry, the killing fields are never too far away as a moral context, not to browbeat the poetic effort but as a kind of vigilant omniscient shadow cast over the frailties and tenacity of the human voice. The stern practitioner and the knowledgeable teacher merge in the powerful vision of *Collected Critical Writings* for the reader to challenge, revise, revisit and review. But the good news is that Geoffrey Hill raises these issues in the very grounds of poetry itself and in so doing raises the standard in our 'techno-culture'.

Three Poets

Roy Campbell famously described the group of middle class, university-educated poets associated with WH Auden as 'Macspaunday'. His distaste for their seemingly unassailable grip on the Thirties literary scene was renowned. While Auden emerged victoriously out of the decade, and the controversies of his moving to America as WW2 was declared, the fate of 'Mac' (Louis Mac Neice), 'Sp' (Stephen Spender) and 'Day' (Cecil Day-Lewis) was much less clear. Spender survived the war, and the fifties, to become a highly regarded critic and chronicler of his generation, very much involved in the intellectual and ideological battles of post-war Britain and its relations with war ravaged Europe and triumphant America, though his poetry drifted from critical view. Mac Neice pursued—if that word fits—a 'career', as an academic and subsequently as a radio producer for the BBC in London, and, as the centenary celebrations at Queen's University Belfast has shown, he survived being forever tagged as the other senior partner in the Auden Generation game. Indeed Mac Neice emerges as one of the greatest English language poets of the mid 20th century: a remarkably adept, subtle, engaged imagination that withstood the pressures and frailties of his time and, perhaps, more importantly, his own personal demons. The wondrous *Collected Poems of Louis Mac Neice* (edited by Peter Mac Donald, 2007) is clear evidence of a poet sticking to his guns, come what may—a lesson in itself for these times. The reputation of the fourth rider of the apocalypse, Cecil Day Lewis, has suffered the most, and in Peter Stanford's new (there only has been one other) biography, we have the chance to wonder why, by revisiting Day-Lewis's life work as a poet.

Peter Stanford, it needs to be said, has done a great job in assembling in *C Day-Lewis: A Life* (2007), the various strands of autobiography that fed Day-Lewis's poetic imagination. The early loss at the age of four of his mother , the unpredictable domineering presence of his Reverend father, the 'Anglo-Irish' background—an obviously key influence on Day-Lewis's sense of self, as all embracing as it was in regard to his friend, Elizabeth Bowen, though he was 'not quite two when his parents left Ballintubbert and Ireland forever, ...ever after he always defined himself, when asked, as Irish'—and a passionate nature, which led him into several complicated and complicating love affairs as a twice-married man, were the makings of both man and poet.

The generational pull of politics and the belief that poetry had to be constantly brought before the public's attention, particularly in the increasingly disinterested fifties and early sixties, brought with it other civic responsibilities: sitting on numerous arts, library and cultural relations committees, as well as the role of English poet laureate. It all reveals a man who, while appearing to be an obvious and very public part of the literary establishment, was actually a man of very deep and unresolved contradictions.

Under the non-de-plume Nicholas Blake, Day-Lewis wrote a series of successful detective novels, including the intensely auto-biographical, *The Private Wound* (1968)—a film script, if ever there was one—set in his beloved west of Ireland, where he and his family spent many summers in Louisburgh, Co Mayo.

His performances, on stage, radio and, towards the end of his life, on television, with his revered second wife, the distinguished actor, Jill Balcon, point to his fervent belief in poetry as a dramatic and popular art. Shy and often introspective, he sang Tom Moore melodies, when given half a chance. Like Mac Neice he lived through the London Blitz but made light of his own contribution to the Home Front war effort; and through his communist activities in the thirties, he had been monitored by MI5.

As Stanford's moving account of this goodly man moves towards his final months, terminally ill, living in the home of

Elizabeth Jane Howard and Kingsley Amis, nursed by his wife, and visited by his dear friends, such as Auden, the biographer reports an exchange with Jill. It's January 1972: 'judged too ill to travel to the BBC Television Centre in west London…crew and performers gathered in the Day-Lewises' sitting room—along with emergency generators because a miners' strike was threatening power cuts. One evening after filming, when the lights had gone off again, Balcon was making a fire in the study. As he sat watching her, he remarked, as if recalling his youth, "I'm always on the side of the miners"'.

On the strength of this detailed account of his life, it seems that Day-Lewis was on the side of the angels. And for that he, like his poetry, should be praised. John Betjeman's 'verdict' was certainly clear: 'I am absolutely sure his poetry was underrated. He persists in the mind. I just rattle on the ears'. In revisiting some of the houses in which Day-Lewis had lived, Stanford remarks that the poet 'had a great capacity to respond to new places and new landscapes…but he never truly settled, physically or emotionally, however much part of him yearned for it. Each paradise was always, as he admitted, lost, often through his own actions. One side of him remained forever the traveller of his poems'- an insight amply dramatised by Stanford's important and necessary study.

For a man born in 1902 (only a couple of years earlier than Day-Lewis), Patrick MacDonogh should look, one feels, older somehow, of another age, as for instance Patrick Kavanagh does with those ancient spectacles and crumpled countryman's overcoat and hat. The photograph on the back cover of Patrick MacDonogh's *Poems* (2001), edited with an introduction by Derek Mahon, shows a contemporary face—alert, ironic, intense and vulnerable. MacDonogh looks very much of the here and now, resisting any effort to historically 'place' him as belonging to the past. Derek Mahon remarks in his introduction:

> Obsessed with youth and novelty, we sometimes patronise previous generations, imagining them to have been more naïve than they were; for, of course, everything has been done or thought before in one form or another, though our historical provincialism tends to ignore the fact. We patronise, too, their difficult achievements.

MacDonogh's achievement as a poet is based upon five collections of poetry: *Flirtation* (1927), *A Leaf in the Wind* (1929), *The Vestal Fire* (1941), *Over the Water* (1943), and *One Landscape Still and Other Poems* (1958) which was 'in effect a collected poems', according to Mahon. The Gallery Press edition drops eleven poems from *One Landscape Still* and adds eight 'including six "new" poems from MacDonogh's brief final period, 1957-1961'. So what we have is MacDonogh's poetic output in seventy pages.

It is a very troubled voice that comes through these poems, a voice that poetry in Ireland is not fully accustomed to hearing, given the predominantly social concerns of so much modern Irish poetry. MacDonogh's tone of voice, when he is not imitating the bardic or mimicking Yeats, has a shriving, analytical and (frankly) tragic timbre:

> ...staring in at the same old questions,
> Never pretend that convictions of truth,
> Those prizes of ignorance, can be won again
> With all the knowing solutions of youth,
> But turn to each other, glad of the reality,
> And accept the pain.

In 'Make Believe', from which the above quotation comes, MacDonogh refers to 'the house opposite us/As that shack in the forest, our Enchanted Castle, /Long before these troubles.' The double inflection of 'our Enchanted Castle' and 'these troubles' plays like a pulse throughout *Poems* because, as Derek Mahon remarks,' there was, and remained, something lost-domanish about MacDonogh's sensibility' along with 'a subject more fully developed later—that of essential solitude.'

What both the solitude and 'lost-domainish'-ness point to is 'a crisis of sensibility, an examination not of conscience but of consciousness' which MacDonogh's editor interprets as a 'morbid unspontaneity—the "original sin", so to speak, in the Protestant soul—is scrutinised with self-conscious unsponstaneity.'

Mahon alludes to the personal roots that lie behind this crisis: 'MacDonogh fell prey to psychiatric problems and spent increasing periods in mental hospitals' and it is a disturbance which carries into the poetry:

The rust is on the lilac bloom
And on the hinges of my mind
Break in upon that quiet room,
Pull back the curtains, lift the blind—
Victorian brass all tarnished now,
Worm in the good mahogany.
Come, most meticulous *hausfrau*,
Refurbish all there's left to see.

The landscape of his poems is not surprisingly a haunted one, wherein the house, enchanted or otherwise, stands in for a permanent familiar world no longer accessible. For this athletic cosmopolitan, with a doctorate on William Allingham, enterprising executive for Guinness (and co-founder of the original Irish festival, the Galway Oyster Festival), driving fast cars, professional man about town, was badly torn by 'a vaguely guilt-ridden detachment [which] he seems to have considered endemic to the Protestant situation'.

Dogged by a morbid sense of isolation, despite job and family, he tried to escape this, in life, through manic activity of various kinds—and, in the work, by embodying the rupture between subject and object, perceiver and perceived, text and context, in highly wrought formal structures.

The Beckett reference fits because MacDonogh shared with his famous contemporary a social and moral universe which has by now almost completely vanished but which provided (if that is the right word) a unique grasp of the physical and inner world and the individual's struggle therein:

This morning I wakened among loud cries of seagulls
Thronging in misty light above my neighbour's ploughland,
And the house in its solid acres was carried wheeling
Encircled in desolate waters and impenetrable cloudy
Wet winds that harried and lost the sea-birds' voices
And the voice of my darling, despairing and drowning,
Lost beyond finding [.]

Patrick MacDonogh is a very fine poet but like others of his generation he has drifted from view. Perhaps we are only now in a position to critically appreciate the divergences that make up

'Irish poetry' and the men and women who wrote and published their books in Dublin, Belfast, London and further afield, between the Twenties and the beginnings of the poetry boom which started just a little after MacDonogh's untimely death in 1961.

In a preface to *Poetry Ireland Review* (winter, 2001) Maurice Harmon suggested that there was a loss or diminution of vision in contemporary Irish poetry. His observation was clearly without malice and it was intended, if I read him correctly, as a note of guidance, not complaint:

> There seems to be a preference at present for poetry in which the pressure of ideas is not a factor. There is nothing wrong with this in itself, but it seems so much is being left out. The thoughtful poem is hard to find these days.

The understanding that a book of poems can be shaped and given an imaginative pattern is also becoming a thing of the past. The interlinking and crafting of a poetic order—be that in visual terms, tone of voice, an aesthetic—is more often than not viewed, when seen at all, with suspicion.

Poems must stand on their own individual ground. They must have some distinct inner value of sound, of creating an image; this we know. But there is a sense in which the power of association, the accumulation of these sounds and images bring an added dimension to a poet's work when it is gathered into a single 'volume'. That added dimension is elusive and it cannot be manufactured at will. The reviewer (and reader) whose appetite is more for the quick hit can miss it all together.

One has to bear in mind, however, the context in which such an observation is made. Contemporary Irish poetry is written and published more or less in a critical vacuum. What responses there are depend more today than ever before upon how the individual poet's work is received *outside* the country—a reception which in turn is predicated upon whether or not the work is published in England or the US.

In general the nature of critical attention is foreshortened by the exigencies of space and the (relatively) limited audience for poetry. With informed coverage on radio increasingly rare and precious little in the national and Sunday "quality" newspapers, poetry's status as a minority interest has meant that poetry reviewing is fast disappearing.

Michael Hartnett, one of the finest contemporary poets, had this condition under surveillance for quite some time. He was, after all, an astute observer of the rhetorical place of poetry in Irish society and knew more than most about the power bases of language—English and Irish of course, but other continental languages as well, including Spanish. He also clocked the vagaries of the writing life and maintained an unfazed understanding of precisely what, when the chips were down, poetry actually means to the wider society. The marvellous Pat Collins 'Necklace of Wrens' (1999) documentary profile of Hartnett illustrates the point.

I think too that Hartnett displayed a vibrant stoicism and ironic edge in the best of his work which is also in danger of being packaged for easier consumption. The other side of this energy is his pure lyrical grace, particularly in his love poetry, such as *Poems to Younger Women* (1988). While it passed by with not much of a stir, *The Killing of Dreams* (1992) is another such perfect "little" book, embodying the kind of prismatic clarity that is a hallmark of Hartnett's work in English. *The Killing of Dreams* reads like stock-taking, engaged by and in the issues already raised here. It is a meditation on poetry and poets in Hartnett's characteristically wry and sometimes hurt manner of speaking. It also reveals a poetic imagination at one with itself but at odds with the world it inhabits. A constitutional unease, let it be said, part of the poet's own self, and not something prepared for the moment.

Small wonder that there has been throughout Hartnett's poetry a persistent feeling that the poet is a fugitive figure who dons various (Poundian) disguises and defences. From his own bi-linguialism to his versions of *Tao* (1972) and translation from Lorca's *Gypsy Ballads* (1973), Hartnett has demonstrated a great facility with language. He seems to know that the language which he talks and thinks in as a poet yearns for some kind of authority which is no longer available. Hartnett also ironically chastises such aspirations.

There is quite a lot going on behind the chaste and amenable facades of Hartnett's poetry. An icy acceptance, for instance, that the incidental, unexpected and idiosyncratic can yield imaginative truth. This kind of realism produces it own anger and rage like the kind of curse which concluded *A Farewell to English* (1975):

I have made my choice
And leave with little weeping:
I have come with meagre voice
To court the language of my people.

In *The Killing of Dreams* Hartnett shifted the register towards an even more personal key. The collection, one of the most intriguing volumes, published in the 1990s, is as much a lament as it is an *ars poetica*.

The Killing of Dreams has also an added twist. In 'Talking Verses' the poem itself strikes back, mocking the poet who earlier in the book has taken himself and his art too seriously for the poem's own good. The poem insists:

I have survived the tribal scar,
The decorative tattoo.
What I say is what I am
And is not open to tirades from you:
Trying not not to be is what I do.

The poem's resistance could well turn out to be a radical thing. What never ceases to impress me about this volume of Hartnett's is just how fleet of foot it is: ironic, emotionally charged, visually strong, conversational, depth-charged and funny. Not bad for fifteen poems or, if you prefer, thirty odd pages of verse. This impression has also been strengthened by recent readings of the poems in their new setting in the *Collected Poems* (2001) edited by Peter Fallon. The opening canto of the closing poem, 'Mountains, Fall on Us' conveys this liveliness and grotesquerie in one unfolding scene:

Outside the Easter air was full of drums
and penitents swayed by
with Christs on catafalques
and one man-fearing man at the café door
blew to him a loud and squeaking kiss.
This brought him back to earth,
back to the Confraternity bands
with their jeering trumpets.
In the hooded hostile street,
away from his sea mosaics,

away from his rightful place.
With a handkerchief white-winged
like a seagull in his hands
some waiter kindly dabbed
the distraught mascara from his face.

For while a few of the poems might be said to veer a little too close to the strain of the sentimental, the dominant force of Hartnett's poetry in English, with *The Killing of Dreams* at the centre, depicts a tragi-comedy as austere, as troubled and as pure as Beckett's prose. Again the following is from 'Mountains, Fall on Us', canto 5:

And now I sit forsaken and stood up
in a no-star eating-house,
a one-armed bandit hurdy-gurdying out
the same synthetic notes,
where the floorboards wear their patina of dirt
as tourists wear a fading tan,
as the overhead electric fan
cuts slices from the curdling smoke
and garlic curses clatter in the kitchens.
Not for me the poet's gold Dimaratos
stood up and staring at a plastic rose:
I am living now in one of his more real fictions.

Is this fine achievement passing us by? If so, possibly further indication of how forty years of a truly ingenious poet's work and vision, shaped and honed with the concentration of a sculptor, can be (at best) misheard and (at worse) overlooked. Michael Hartnett himself had the last laugh in *The Killing of Dreams*. It is though such a pity that he is not around to continue into his sixties, seventies and eighties where *The Killing of Dreams* and the subsequent volumes left off. With the bright temptation of a colossal Gaelic and European tradition at his back and the wicked knowledge of the contemporary world all around to give him food for thought, Michael Hartnett embodied the modern complications of the Irish poetic and, what is so important, he gave them voice.

Travels

i

In Amsterdam you can walk without fear most places, the people smile and respond to queries in precise English: a courteous, decent people. The rivers sluice their sandy streets, but something, maybe a sense of growth, seems missing even while the entire city is coming down with history. You look about expecting completeness but find instead a marvellous miniature, like a child's toy house that verges between the nightmarish and the self-engrossed; the unreal and the tranquil. There is something extraordinarily artificial about Amsterdam.

Everything is in its right place. The canals decrease by semi-circles towards the sea; the dogs step politely on their owner's leads; the police look immaculate in their speeding vans and everyone seems to know everyone else on the street-side cafés. In the midst of all this decorum, equally well run, is the Red Light District, notorious the world over, like an Island of Sin in a city of great parables concerning Europe's history.

It was in Amsterdam in 1981 that I picked up D M Thomas's translation of the twentieth century Russian poet, Anna Akhmatova. In the Athenaeum bookshop, in fact, while William Burroughs signed autographs of his re-released books, sitting within a group of gleaming, large-bespectacled Dutch; I rooted around upstairs and found *Way of All the Earth* (1978).

Some books wait for their reader like an ambush, for the unsuspecting person. This certainly happened to me before, with the Penguin book of Akhmatova's poetry, published in 1969. I was captivated by the exquisite poise of her poetry, the range and clarity, the strength of what DM Thomas calls in his introduction to *Way of All the Earth*, 'the encompassing of the serious and the popular within one voice':

> Why is our century worse than any other?
> Is it that in the stupor of fear and grief
> It has plunged its fingers in the blackest ulcer,
> Yet cannot bring relief?
>
> Westward the sun is dropping,
> And the roofs of towns are shining in its light.
> Already death is chalking doors with crosses
> And calling the ravens and the ravens are in flight.

These lines are separated from us by more than seventy years, yet those intervening decades amount to nothing, given that timeless power to communicate, even through the sea change of another language.

Coming back late after a reading in a small remote town, I couldn't settle. The neon of the hotel burned below my window; the air was chilly, the sound of cars swishing to a halt outside the Concert Hall as the musicians headed home and the gasping whine of a police siren made it impossible to relax into the kind of drowsiness that brings sleep. So with pillows stacked up behind me, the window wide open, the buzz of the hotel's neon and the white strip-light above my head, I sank into Akhmatova's poetic world, her passion and grief, and the English Thomas had made out of it:

> In the young century's cool nursery.
> In its chequered silence, I was born.
> Sweet to me was not the voice of man,
> But the wind's voice was understood by me.
> The burdocks and the nettles fed my soul,
> But I loved the silver willow best of all,
> And, grateful for my love, it lived

All its life with me, and with its weeping
Branches fanned my insomnia with dreams. But
Surprisingly enough!—I have outlived
It. Now, a stump's out there. Under these skies,
Under these skies of ours, are other
Willows, and their alien voices rise.
And I am silent ... As though I'd lost a brother.

Stuck in the middle of that precisely ornamented European town,
I began to merge into another world of lucidity, where poetry had
a power all of its own. There was nothing cramped or churlish
about this particular world, growing out of the shadowy transience
of one October, many years ago:

Black and enduring separation
I share equally with you.
Why weep? Give me your hand,
Promise me you will come again.
You and I are like high
Mountains and we can't move closer.
Just send me word
At midnight sometimes through the stars.

But the worlds I was hearing were busily subdued voices rummaging
for keys, a high-pitched giggle, the solace of the morning already
beginning to make itself felt; the cool breeze buffeting the curtains
and that anonymity only hotel-rooms possess. I had read for most
of the night without noticing the time and had plunged repeatedly
through the book:

Here I can see the sun rise earlier
And see the glory of the day's end.
And often into the window of my room
Fly the winds of a northern sea,
A dove eats wheat from my hands ...
And the Muse's sunburnt hand
Divinely finishes the unfinished page.

Prague is one of those places you dream about. I certainly have had the Czech capital in mind since I read Kafka's diaries and his novels such as *The Castle* and *The Trial*. As a teenager I had fancied travelling through the Sixties in what was called 'East Europe'; meeting up with great writers in spectacular landscapes, traversing an historical otherworld on exotic railways, light-years away from the encroaching habits of home. Then something quite shocking happened when, in 1969, the young student Jan Palach set himself on fire in St. Wenceslas Square in protest at the Russian invasion and the ensuing closure of the borders between Czechoslovakia and the outside world. It seemed a terrible thing to let happen.

I thought of that time, thirty year later, when I was in Prague staying in an ex-Communist Party hotel—it was more like a dormitory—close by the graveyard where the young man is buried. His Czechoslovakia has gone now, split into two separate republics. In the palace, the playwright president, Vaclav Havel took up residence above the dreamy city which, going by the number of billboards and display cards, has been taken over by American big business.

From the first day I arrived in the hotel lobby when I overheard three intense young business men, talking in Czech and English, discuss the pros and cons of a finance deal concerning mobile phones, it seemed that half of Prague was being bought and sold and business, the market economy, was on everyone's mind. No wonder. The years of communist rule had been an unqualified disaster but even the disaster had some upturns. The architectural marvel of Prague was preserved in bureaucratic aspic. Now, there is a heady rush to embrace what are seen as the monetarist miracles that have been evangelised throughout Europe. To question the social and cultural impact of the gluttony of market-driven forces is heresy in such a country, deprived of decent standards of living (not to speak of civic rights) as were so many of the eastern European countries in the post-WWII period.

Indeed, contemporary society throughout continental Europe is awash with the managerial spirit of market economics. The Poles I spoke with, the Hungarians, Slavs, all were speaking the same language we have been hearing in Ireland since the late

1980s. The social vacuum caused by the collapse of communism has been filled with the jargon of privatisation and the mantra of American populist culture. How the people are responding is difficult to know. The inescapable starkness of the contrast between our self-inflicted wounding in Ireland and the pervasive oppressiveness of eastern European life was as plain as a pikestaff.

iii

Why is it that there is no end to the changes taking place at London's Heathrow airport? Is there some kind of congenital need for the management at said airport to confuse the long-suffering public with constantly rewritten directions of how one should progress from one terminal to another? The thought stayed with me on the flight to Poland to participate in the Lodz Seminar on Contemporary Poetry. Along with Nuala Ni Dhomhnaill, Craig Raine, Christopher Reid, Katherine Pierpoint and the Polish writers Piotr Summer, Bohdan Zadura, and Jerzy Jarniewicz and under the energetic supervision of the then- Lodz-based poet, Cathal McCabe, I spent five unforgettable days in Poland.

The journey to Lodz took us through a murky evening. The darkness is from the night air as much as from the obscure lamplight. We travelled through flat lands and few villages and towns to reach Lodz as a dusting of snow fell on the previous week's spring snow. The long wide avenue is lit-up and the young are embracing each other, heading into bars and restaurants and the occasional hotel.

Like other countries in what was once the 'Eastern bloc', Poland is rushing forwards to catch up with the rest of Europe. Behind the main streets, and oftentimes, on them as well, the facades of old buildings crumble away, unmaintained. Factories in the once thriving industrial centre of Lodz stand idle in their own grounds. The old Communist Party hotels, like the Grand, sport a new rising class of entrepreneurs eager to shake the dust of the past off their heels.

Poetry was everywhere, from the Angel Bar on the opening night of the seminar, with intent young faces framed in a club which belonged somehow to the Sixties (with bedstead, bicycle, radiogram and the eschewed portrait of Lenin: had he a red-lipped kiss on his cheek or was I seeing things?) to the setting of the Teachers' Club, table-cloths, mirrors and fireplaces, high ceilings and the sense of generations of mental fight and waiting. The Poles speak with intimate formality. It sounds like a language of great elegance and, as Bohdan Zadura exhibited in his reading, of satirical mirth. Guesswork is the privilege of the stranger.

One undoubted highlight was meeting with Jadwiga and Januisz Tyrzno in the villa where Rubenstein played in what is now a dilapidated drawing room but with impeccable acoustics still. The villa houses Correspondance des Arts, their printing works, and the Tryzno team have a stunning vision of converting the entire site into a grand art museum of The Book. A brilliant idea which needs economic and diplomatic support through EU intervention for not only is the Museum a project to help technologically and practically the makers and artists of the Book throughout Europe; it will reassert how culturally coherent the diverse strands are which make up the literal history of the continent. A hope reinforced by our last day.

Before returning, we stopped at the Jewish Cemetery in Lodz. Its demesne walls seemed to stretch for miles before we turned in off the main road and entered via the narrow iron door *bet hachayim*, 'house of the living'. Acres of headstones like rocks on a beach, record the names and occupations of those who have passed on; delicate images inscribed on headstones that are returning to nature. But nothing can assuage the terrible un-voiceable shock of the Ghetto Field where the lives of the Lodz Jews are foregathered and the six pits, dug by and for them to perish in, line a peripheral wall. This dispersal of the Jews was almost final. Cathal McCabe, in his poem, 'A Letter from Lodz', replays the following lines from Oskar Rosenfield, who after the liquidation of the Lodz ghetto in August 1944, was deported to Auschwitz:

> This week forty years ago
> A further frantic search began
> For those who would indeed be sent
> 'To work in the Generalgouvernement',
> Finish up in Buchenwald. In the Beginning
> Was the Ghetto.

Five days proves nothing but gives an inkling of what needs to be done as countries and cultures throughout Europe converge and question what the past was like and what the future may hold.

iv

If you haven't read D H Lawrence's travel essays you should. Lawrence isn't much in critical favour these days even though his novels and short stories are never out of print. His travel essays are provocative snapshots of the places he visited and often set up home in after leaving his native England with Frieda Weekley more or less for good in 1919. A few years earlier he published *Twilight in Italy*, a collection of essays dealing with his travels in southern Europe just on the brink of the Great War. The closing essay, 'The Return Journey' is based on Lawrence's walking tour—and I do mean *walking* tour—of part of Switzerland as he recounts his journey from overlooking Zurich to approaching Milan. It is an unsettling journey for many reasons. The people he meets en route, fellow travellers, are themselves unsettled and Lawrence views many of the locals as neurotics, displaced in some cases; troubled as much as the time and pace of events. The following (edited) passage gives an idea of what he is going on about:

> Emerging through the dark rocky throat of the pass I came to the upper world, the level upper world. It was evening, livid, cold. The twilight deepened, though there was still the strange, glassy translucency of the snow-lit air. A fragment of moon was in the sky. A carriage-load of French tourists passed me. There was the loud noise of water, as ever, something eternal and maddening in its sound, like the sound of Time itself, rustling and rushing and wavering, but never for a second ceasing. The rushing of Time that continues throughout eternity, this is the sound of the icy streams of Switzerland, something that mocks and destroys our warm being.

Lawrence decides to stay the night but before retiring to his room he has a late supper:

I sat in the utter isolation and stillness, eating bread and drinking the wine, which was good. And I listened for any sound: only the faint noise of the stream. And I wondered, Why am I here, on this ridge of the Alps, in the lamp-lit, wooden, close-shut room, alone? Why am I here? Yet somehow I was glad, I was happy even: such splendid silence and coldness and clean isolation. It was something eternal, unbroachable: I was free, in this heavy, ice-cold air, this upper world, alone. London, far away below, beyond, England, Germany, France—they were all so unreal in the night. It was a sort of grief that this continent all beneath was so unreal, false, non-existent in its activity. Out of the silence one looked down on it, and it seemed to have lost all importance, all significance. It was so big, yet it had no significance. The kingdoms of the world had no significance: what could one do but wander about?

In the morning Lawrence breakfasted and leaves for Italy. I remember reading that essay many years ago and I thought that one day I should like to visit the country and see for myself. Luckily over the recent past I have had the chance to visit Switzerland on a few occasions and spend some time there. For a visitor any place can only ever be seen from the outside. That stands to reason. But having time to stay in the one place and observe how life is lived around you has some benefits.

For a start, Switzerland is a political achievement of deliberate and enlightened reason—and perhaps rezoning. Surrounded by five states—France, Germany, Austria, Italy and little Liechtenstein—the country is an historical balancing act of cultural and religious difference. The cantons and communes, which make up the civic constitution of this most civil of nations, embody Switzerland's landscape of language with mutual care.

The somewhat serious train conductors will adjust their address at the drop of a frown or look of perplexity—from French to German (or the Swiss versions of both) to Italian and even to English. I have not experienced elsewhere in Europe such practical assistance at railway stations as the un-vexable staff that smile all-knowingly at my blabbering enquiries and explain the excellent, reliable and rational network, which is justifiably Switzerland's pride and joy.

Quite simply you can go in Switzerland just about everywhere—up high, very high, and low down, out of the way or main line—by train. It is a true revelation for an Irish traveller to recognise at first hand a transport *system* geared to the citizen. An expectation ground in everyday assumptions that the railway system—and its integration with bus and ferry—is what the state provides for the people, not as an afterthought, nor as a necessary evil but as a right! Comfort, cleanliness, reliability, diversity and choice: imagine. Despite the best will of all those trusty souls who in Ireland do their best, we are still in the dark ages of public transport. Just imagine a kindervagen (a kids' carriage with slides and bouncing castles) on the Galway-Dublin line! A substantial part of my joy in being in Switzerland is travelling by train.

Take the line from St Gallen (on the German side) to Lausanne (on the French). It is pricey to use (although if you are in Switzerland for any length of time the Swiss travel card offers great deductions) but it is spellbinding, traversing the countryside. This route is fairly run-of-the-mill in comparison with some of the truly spectacular journeys you can map out for yourself in, up and around the Alps and the lakes.

I'm not all that keen on such elevated sight seeing. I prefer ground level. The regional train that takes you from Lausanne to Brig suddenly exits a tunnel and there on your left hammer is the magnificent, earth defying beauty of Lake Geneva, Lac Leman, overseen by the glory of Mont Blanc. Such views are visions of a kind that you will never forget. Certainly the great Romantic poets Byron and Shelley didn't; nor T S Eliot on a spot of recuperation who recalls in *The Waste Land*: 'By the waters of Leman I sat down and wept'. While several writers have commented on the chocolate-boxy beauty of the country and on the somewhat introverted and serious nature of the Swiss, I can't for the life of me complain. Their unassuming respect for the land and cityscapes leaves our filthy streets, unplanned rural developments and woeful yellow-pack contemporary architecture for dead. Fussy maybe they are, but the Swiss can teach us all a thing or two about design and about how to maintain the historical fabric of the physical world in which we live, rather than demolishing whatever gets in the way of 'development'.

Their systems for recycling all kinds of waste, their knacky ways of making the most out of limited domestic space; the manner in which they honour their own people and their ability to make up their own minds about where they stand on issues of European neutrality and integration is refreshing. Whatever about the pools of anxiety and anguish which undoubtedly reside under the surface of life in Switzerland—rising alcoholism and serious drug abuse, formidable psychic tensions, dubious (to say the least) banking practises in regard to stolen Jewish wealth from WW2—the Swiss get by with style and civic care. French Swiss, German Swiss, Italian Swiss and the increasing numbers of migrant workers seeking a life in the landlocked country from which all of Europe is only a train ride away.

It is a country, which has great pride in its local roots and celebrates its rural and folk traditions with real energy; that sees visual art as a central and necessary part of popular culture, along with its unselfconscious and sophisticated enjoyment of classical music and jazz from street festival to city concert hall. If things can get "kitchy", well, so what? Ever watched Dutch, Belgian, German, or Italian TV with those excruciating "entertainment" programmes that go on for hours on end? A couple of years ago a fellowship took me to the Writers' Foundation in Martigny, in the hills over-looking Lake Geneva. In the discreet chateau that had been the home of a well known German publisher, a handful of Greek, German, English, Mexican and Egyptian writers gathered. While working there I realised that I was intrigued by Switzerland and its cultural and religious echoes and by the responses to the country of great writers such as Henry James who sets the opening of his story, *Daisy Miller* on the lake. Faced with the beauty of the landscape any one will succumb but for how long, before that return journey beckons?

V

The senior poet danced by me: 'Greenland, Greenland', and he was gone. It was the real place we were flying over; not the imagined territory associated forever (and much to his chagrin) with

Graham Greene. I didn't stir. I had hit that mid-flight time in my head when ennui and tiredness and a kind of irritability bounce like electrons inside the body on a long (longish) haul flight.

The west coast of Canada isn't so very far away after all—a day's work away, if you like—but the trouble, of course, is not the long day's journey from Dublin via Heathrow to Vancouver but the time shift. Cosseted with blankets, ear phones, little pillows, eye shades, in-flight entertainment, food, more food, a couple of little bottles of wine, plastic glasses of water, and the surrounding darkness, flying is a little like being in the cinema. Except that there is something vaguely sacred about it too: unasked-for closeness, like being in church. People you don't know at all talk close by and intimately to one another; go to the bathroom, read under their individual night-light. Now, of course, they also patrol the aisles in the aerobically fashionable act of exercising their bodies. And they all drink those little cups of water in the strange ceremonial evening of the perpetual night flight.

I was cagey. At London City airport, my Mach razors were confiscated before a flight back from London to Dublin, although I could only have injured myself in trying to use such a thing as a weapon. The truth is that post September 11th everyone is on edge, looking or pretending not to look at each other in a special intent way. Can it be helped?

I confess my own heart skipped a beat when a couple of passengers engaged in heated conversation. Two English passengers on board the BA flight sitting in front of me were obviously highly animated when another passenger spent quite a bit of time in the loo right beside us. He emerged, resumed his seat and slept the remainder of the journey. Prejudice, no, I think not. But fearfulness, yes.

Any Irish man or woman well knows what it was like in the bad old days of the 1970s and 80s when the security men heard the accent, checked the passport and clocked Belfast written there. A second look, another keying into the computer; a hastier, frostier, more "something" encounter; or was it just in our own heads? Is it any wonder, given the horror of September 11 that we look at each other with a different kind of anxiety, anger, shame, uncertainty, bravado, resignation, and understanding? It's hard to know. Flying is all about trust. It still amazes me that the whole thing works in the first place. This might be a cultural gene I inherited from my great grandmother who refused to accept the fact that there definitely were not real people in the radio box. I still feel ever so slightly silly sitting up there above the clouds, having a bite to eat, watching a movie, listening to the earth-bound news-stories on the headset.

Aviation is a magnificent human achievement. Getting hundreds of people off the ground in comfort, looking after their welfare in such a confined and lethal space, getting them back down safely again, all of them, all those aeroplanes all over the world, criss-crossing with their precious human cargo—it is mind-boggling.

I lost track of where we were and went for my own walkabout. The cabin windows were mostly closed but my attention was drawn to one empty row whose shutter was half way open, with sunlight streaming in. Sitting cross-legged at the window seat, a Sikh (I think) was in prayer or meditation. I could have hugged him, with his half-lit face, his tranquillity, and his self-possession. Instead I kept walking by the rows of sleeping bodies, practising what I was told would be good for my own well being. Greenland had passed by; Canada beckoned. I saw snowy space as far as my mind's eye could see, sleepwalking in the kind of no man's land we inhabit in time travels.

vi

Japan is quite simply like no other place I've ever been to; it's utterly compelling and I can see why the country transfixes Europeans. Certainly the French whose first class Air France shuttle back and forth every day suggests as much. Nothing can quite prepare you for the amazing site of Tokyo—mega-metropolis, stretching for miles and miles and miles. A vertical city. An underground city. An endless city. Yet life goes on with courtesy, indeed ceremonial courtesy, good humour and common decency despite the sheer crush. Polite to a fault. But the numbers! Thankfully my guide through the extensive, proliferating railway system was Dublin born poet and Kinsella expert, Andrew Fitzsimons, who read the signs of the times, places and platforms like a wizard. 'It takes time to get used to the different lines'. A lifetime I'd say. Underground takes on a new meaning when you're underground in Tokyo. Five floors down I began to get the heebie-jeebies, but then when you're 40 floors up and more, gazing across the horizon of skyscrapers, coordination goes out the window. Earth, air; sky become utterly relative. Look. I can walk in the clouds! Or I can visit the bowels of the earth, which is what 2,710 people, did when they trekked 1.46 kilometers along the underground tunnel system of what is known as the Azabu-Hibiya Common Utility Duct.

According to a newspaper report, this underground Parthenon attracts an ever-increasing number of excursions as visitors are taken on a guided tour, 35-40 metres down, through a vast network of gargantuan tunnels. When completed the tunnels will form 'a vast high-tech catacombs' housing flood control sewers, and utility lines such as telephone, electricity and gas.

With a population of 12 million in what could be called inner city Tokyo, and a population of 30 million in the metropolitan area, no wonder there's a parallel universe underground to service it all. As E M Forster had it, let's hope the machine never stops. And if Hachiko Square is anything to go by nothing will ever stop—reputedly the busiest crossing in the world, the day I negotiated the Square it seemed as if Japan's 125 million people were out window-shopping under the Q-Front Building.

But numbers never really tell the story. There are the sleeping figures of the businessmen and women on Shinkansen (bullet trains) as they shoot across the island; mobile phones are required to be switched off so silence reigns. Imagine that: a train without the ceaseless gabbiness of soundbites. And then there's the rubbish, or I should say, the lack of it. The spectral Yamamba (Mountain Crone) Girls, a peacock flare of colour, idling on the platforms, the incredible dapper bespoke young men, the endless chorus of schoolgirls, of whom there is a cult, heading fearlessly to and fro across the city.

The Great Buddha at Kamakura cast in 1252 AD sits in his hillside brooding with magnificent magnanimity while people stand prayerfully before him, as if he had fallen from the sky, a chastening reminder of all that is good and holy. And the temples; the temples. Shrines. Gardens. Jozan Ishikawa (1583-1672), landscape architect, scholar of Chinese classics, one time samurai, created in Shisen-do a simple place of immeasurable peace. Buddhist priests are now the custodians. The house contains along with its main rooms, study and garden, a Shogetsuro, a small moon-viewing room. Such infinite sense.

A day spent at the Noh sounds strange to say. But as I muttered to my host, translator and scholar, Nobuaki Tochigi, the extraordinarily stylized folk art, with its ceremonial movement, hypnotic intoning and drumbeat, had me in thrall to I know not what; the passage to some previously uninhabited inner space where dragons and devils, clowns and princes, heroes and villains played on the mind with wonder and fear.

Around the lake in Kyoto, the sun had come out. What looked like fishing pots bobbed out in the middle distance and for a split-second I felt the timelessness of this place. Rain on bamboo, the clack of the water-work scarecrow, the imperial palace, the smiling eager talk of three young Buddhist priests and the preoccupied girl, holding open her umbrella, cycling to work in the hazy morning.

II

Catching the Light
with Niall McGrath

NMG: *There is a preoccupation in your early poems with* destinations. *Do you see this as a Calvinist influence from your background?*

GD: I would never have thought of Calvin. No. Destinations?

NMG: *Some of the poems also refer to being in Presbyterian church halls. Wasn't that part of your background?*

GD: I don't think any of my work is consciously looking for *destination* or has any sense of going somewhere. I have tried to write poems that are like Victorian silhouettes. Clearly etched and edged in. You get that kind of stillness and clarity when you go into a church. But there aren't many poems about churches.

NMG: *Maybe because in* Sheltering Places *you were moving from the North to the South of Ireland and...?*

GD: Yes, well now, in *Sheltering Places* that's a different story, because the poems were written when I wasn't sure that I could write. There is an attempt in *Sheltering Places* to respond in some way to the eruption of the Troubles. I think the notion of the Protestant thing came much later on, when I started to think about my background. I'd been very dismissive and critical of it when I was a younger man, in fact I *hated* it. It took me a while to grow out of that and to think a little more sympathetically of where I'd come from.

NMG: *Illness and fragility seem to be recurrent motifs (eg. In 'From Two').*
Do you see physical vulnerability and temporality as major aspects of life?

GD: As a boy I did suffer from asthma and a family break up and moving from one part of town to another. And I was unwell at a certain time in my very young years. Some of that shadows the early poems.

NMG: *In 'Straws in the Wind', in Sunday School, "…night things bombard/ our fragile peace". It's a very personal poem; isn't it about physical vulnerability?*

GD: There's a sense of vulnerability and delicacy behind the domestic poems. I often feel that there's an arrogance that people live in and that people live on, irrespective of troubles, even though the 'now', the present, can be a very delicate time. I was trying to convey fragility about people in 'Straws in the Wind'. Fragility: a sense in which we can ceremonialise ourselves and yet, here's a young baby who was unwell, and maybe we should spend more attention on the here and now, rather than some other kind of ambition, or grand schemes.

NMG: *Why did you first write?*

GD: I didn't bother much submitting to magazines when I first went to University to study literature. Someone asked me for some for the University magazine. Denys Hawthorne of the BBC visited the Uni' and read them and broadcast a few. One thing led to another. But I've always been a little uneasy about the public side of writing.

NMG: *Who do you see as your most important literary influences?*

GD: I just enjoy so many writers it's difficult to pinpoint a few central presences. But if I had to—the most important Irish writer for me is Yeats. I'm very impressed by Eugene Montale. There's a tremendous intelligence at work in his poems, and his sense of *being in the world*—I enjoy that. Montale writes about music and art. There's none of the kind of *confinement* that is often the case in Irish writing; our *cramped* quality. Robert Lowell: I love his *For the Union Dead* and *Near the Ocean*.

NMG: *You don't use traditional forms very often. Do you think they're more or less irrelevant now?*

GD: Oh no! I was reading something recently that Michael Longley, a poet who I admire a lot, has said that he would love to be able to write like Frank O'Hara and by the time he's worked on the poem it becomes a Michael Longley poem. Well, I've often wanted to write like a Ginsberg or a Walt Whitman, those big elaborate lines and so on. And sometimes I've tried it, but it always ends up in this slightly more compressed form. It depends what you're making comparisons with. I wouldn't see myself as being a traditionalist in terms of my attitude to form; yet at the same time I wouldn't see myself as being 'loose'. So I suppose the poems just make their own kind of register, whatever form that may take. They're worked on quite a bit.

NMG: *In 'The Lundys Letter' it says: "You staged the ultimate coup de grace/ For the Union's son turned Republican". You said there was a rebellion against your background at that period…?*

GD: Several people have asked me about that, that it is myself I'm referring to; in fact, the poem's actually addressed to Ronnie Bunting, who was assassinated by loyalists, but who had been at school with us. And I've been thinking about it, maybe I should have identified that fact. I think there are a few of those poems in the middle part of *The Lundys Letter* that are trying to establish a watershed. I didn't know it at the time, but what the poem was really trying to do was gather together my experience in Belfast in the Sixties and try and make some sense of it. And in effect it was a watershed. Having written that poem, and I'm still not 100% happy with the last part of it, I think it freed me of something. Maybe the kind of sombre, one-dimensional quality that I had to break through to move somewhere else. It's not a political poem; it's more like a memoir.

NMG: *It talks of an "amalgam of desperate love/and politics". Are you looking back on that period from a different perspective?*

GD: Yes; though I've always been a little bit worried about this looking back business.

NMG: *The Sixties was a time of social revolution. Yet that poem was written in the more conservative era of the Eighties. How do you view this aspect of it?*

GD: That's spot-on, because part of 'The Lundys Letter' links in with 'Blueprints' in *Sunday School*. I always try to make a book a book, it's interlinked, and one poem feeds off another. I think what I was saying both in 'Lundys' and 'Blueprints' was that in some way those late Sixties—and I'm not being nostalgic or sentimental—that period was the last chance that a lot of people felt they had to change the world, to actually change the reality in which they lived. And of course that's a marvellous sensation.

NMG: *They had optimism; felt they could do something; whereas now, people are more…pragmatic?*

GD: Yes, what happened then, I think, is that that ideal was defeated by the violence here and elsewhere. Here, the physical terrorist violence; but also in Britain by the violence of the Thatcher years. Which I think was devastation. Defeat takes different forms: it take the slow, Chinese drip of the Thatcher reaction or the kind of bloody violence we've experienced in Ireland. There was a kind of naivety about my generation, who thought that they could actually change things, because there are solid realities which you can't move around. It takes some other process. And it has taken us, regrettably, a generation to realize that.

NMG: *In 'A Question of Covenants' you focus on 28th September 1913, that's a year after Ulster Day—when Lord Carson's Solemn League and Covenant was signed in Belfast and across the north. Why?*

GD: It should be 1912. But because of Yeats' poem 'September 1913' none of us proofing picked up the mistake, a rare mistake. But it happens.

NMG: *Carson is seen in this poem as "a stranger to both sides". Is that satirizing or criticizing him because he was in reality a very neurotic and nervous man, despite his resolute public image?*

GD: I don't think he really understood what was going on.

NMG: *He was caught up in a power game?*

GD: Exactly. He was an actor. And he didn't really understand the people here, either Protestant or Catholic. And he certainly didn't understand the whole ethos of the North; but he could turn it to his advantage. So when I used that phrase "a stranger on both sides" I was actually also thinking of the sides of the Lough, north and south, and how that whole kind of thing was endemic. That he didn't really understand what was going on. That was a poem that I was very pleased with. But I wouldn't have got near that poem without A T Q Stewart's *The Ulster Crisis*, which I identified, in the notes.

NMG: *'Carlyle in Ireland' shows "his anger at their disorderly rage" (that of the Irish). But the poetic tone is not condemning. I think it was Terry Eagleton said you've got an "ambivalence of tone", to "shape and point a balance"; do you try not to bear down too critically?*

GD: I think I do, because I think it's too easy to judge. In 'Carlyle in Ireland' I tried to carry through that 19th century sense of rectitude. Of work ethic and so on. And Carlyle was actually sickened by what he saw. Yet because of the rigour of his mind, he felt that any giving in to what he saw on the roads of Ireland (the starving people during the Famine, nothing but skeletons and rags) would be a concession to sentiment. The notion that Carlyle had was—how could they let themselves be like this? So, it was a total misunderstanding of the situation on Carlyle's behalf that he didn't realize these people did not visit this upon themselves, the squalor and poverty. It was visited upon them by a system. I just imagined Carlyle driving through Ireland in his stagecoach and these figures coming out of the shadows haunting his imagination. Because he was a deeply imaginative man. And yet at the same time he couldn't *give* himself to it. Maybe that's an interesting break between the experiences of both countries. And between writers: some of them have a kind of theoretical understanding, who as it were come from the top and look in, whereas those who come from inside and look out, they have different kinds of attitudes. Some of it is pietistic, other times it can be analytical. It's when those two things meet that you have real imaginative power.

NMG: *In Sunday School you focus on the Bright Hour. But surely most Protestants will not be familiar with this concept, even church-going ones?*

GD: What happened was my wife and I were walking up the Donegall Pass in Belfast and there was a small church being demolished. There was a sign outside saying 'The Bright Hour' and it gave the hours exactly when. So I rooted around, I asked a couple of people, and finally I found this definition, that 'The Bright Hour' was a time set aside for meditation, contemplation, in the Protestant faith. I would say it would be Presbyterian. This happened in the shipyard, for instance. Not in a proselytising sense, although maybe some of the men who were not a part of it may have felt that; but there was a time set aside when workers would read the Bible. Anyway, it's just a phrase, a beautiful phrase—the Bright Hour. I suppose it's been lost; I suppose the quality of the phrase has been compromised now by phrases like the Happy Hour, when drink's cheaper. I suppose men and women did go into this little church hall and sat there. And I just thought that, it wasn't the poignancy, it was the commitment, which I thought was significant.

NMG: *'Dead Men's Shoes' has deeper resonance, suggesting following in the footsteps of previous generations. It mentions a 'call of nature' that you think will put a stop to people's "Walking / the way they were told to"— do you see that some of the Protestant heritage is being eroded? In the past they were brought up and told to do and think things, it was the done thing, and they were afraid not to; but in more recent times people are less anxious about "ruining sacred truths"?*

GD: Exactly. Very few people have really got into the soil of all this. For the Protestant in the north, or at any rate in the Belfast that I grew up in, it was very imperative... there was certain things you did and certain things you didn't do. And it was proverbial; it was based around proverbs and so on. I don't think there was anything wrong with it, but that was the way you did things. And I think what that poem is saying is, it's a dramatic monologue really, whereby the young boy who's remembering or talking about this life, *didn't* do the things he was supposed to do and is breaking for cover, is breaking to get free of *properness*—that in some way was emasculating him. The 'call of nature' is of course going for a pee, but it's also the call of that other nature, the nature of the culture, which constantly calls you back to itself.

NMG: *Something to do with the Jesuit idea of 'give me the child until he is seven': you're programmed culturally?*

GD: Yes.

NMG: *And perhaps the idea that people become more conservative as they get older?*

GD: Well, I don't think I've become more conservative, I hope not. What 'Dead Men's Shoes' is specifically about is that when the past becomes personalized to a family friend who offers her dead husband's shoes, beautiful Oxford shoes,– would you like to wear them—when you're ten years of age? There's something ghastly, honourable and scary all at the same time about that. There's a complex kind of relationship that you have to the past. I was trying to capture that.

NMG: *And some of the images in the whole collection, like on a Saturday watching football and making a cup of tea, that's "the passion that cries out of the ordinary"—it's not so much about religion as what everyday life is like, as if a secular sacredness? And connected to the religion of the tribe: if you're knocking about and it's not Sunday people ask, 'Why aren't you working?'*

GD: Yes, I think that's true. Maybe that world has passed, I don't know. Certainly my boyhood in Belfast was very much influenced by the sense that every thing had a ritual. Even playing "marleys" [marbles], conkers, all these different games, street games. They all had their own time and the day was broken up into certain things. So I think that what *Sunday School* was trying to do was to log all that. You can only ever be free of something when you've written it out of yourself. And then some other things start to take over. In *Heart of Hearts* different things are happening from what was happening in *Sunday School* which is about a community; but I don't think it is limited to that.

NMG: *In the south of Ireland there's the same kind of tribal thing, where almost everybody's of the same religion. Do you think you feel freer there because you're not part of that background and you don't have the same demands on you and are not weighed down by a shared cultural baggage, as you might have in the North?*

GD: Some people can fit in and feel happy no matter where they are. I love coming home to Belfast; I love being here. But I do have that sense of the past being a limiting one and not an enabling one. So maybe part of the imaginative "project" is to try and convert what was negative into positive and to make that available for others. Because I see the poet as being someone who converts negativities into something positive. And if you can't do that, then your poems are 'in' on themselves, they don't make other realities available. I don't think it's as corny as saying in the south I feel free. I think you carry with you your own burdens, no matter where you go. I'd be writing this stuff even if I were in Crete; you're stuck with it.

NMG: *In 'The Messages' there are people in alcoholic dazes, but the poem talks about a bottle bank. That kind of imagery is quite topical, not many people are writing about environmental issues. Sheltering Places was about landscapes. Do you think that's going to be something more important to you in the future?*

GD: The little suburban detail of the bottle bank was just a lift-off for what that poem was moving into. I've never been able to write about anything unless it meant something to me, so I've never seen myself as being ecologically sound. I think the poems of the late Sixties and early Seventies were about landscapes I was discovering for the first time. I think the poems, which immediately followed, in *Sunday School* and *Heart of Hearts*, were rediscoveries of city life. I don't really see myself as writing to themes or agendas. Anybody who has got a brain in their head is Green, I mean ecologically Green; but as for the poems, I don't know.

NMG: *In 'The Messages' and other poems the town is by the sea. Belfast, Galway, Dún Laoghaire, are places you've lived, but do you see the ocean as an important backdrop?*

GD: I love the sea and coastline and I feel most alive when I'm near the sea. I don't know why. And I'm always drawn towards writing about the sea and the coastline and the relationship between the two. Not rivers, not streams, the sea. There are things that you don't know why. Bünuel, the Spanish film director, said that. In his autobiography, *The Last Sigh*, he talks about things he does without knowing why, and he never will know why. It's just there; it's an imaginative reality. Which is comforting, but also threatening and invigorating and I don't know what subconscious need or allurement I have with the sea and coastlines but it's certainly there and I think that the less I know about it the better.

NMG: *In 'The Bright Hour' there are secular experiences of youth, family that appear to be sacred although it's the everyday—the pious William Bailey Chartres, your great-grandfather, 'three times of a Sunday church' is somehow out of step with the social realities of today?*

GD: Oh, totally. He was possibly the last contact our family had with that kind of belief. Certainly my grandmother and my mother wouldn't have followed along with that kind of pattern. In fact, I grew up in a very secular, liberal environment. So I suppose he's the kind of authority figure in the book. He haunts me a bit. He was a very well known man in Belfast of his time and in a way I'm still fencing with him, over two generations. To try and call him out. And he's there in the background in several poems. I half-respect him, in fact I *do* respect him, yet at the same time I think we would be warring every day of the week if I had've been living in the same house with him.

NMG: *Even in* Sunday School, *you include a poem 'Speedboats 1972' with all those experiences, and you refer to 'an invisible foe'. In 'A Question of Covenants' the sea is 'invisible'. Are you using the Christian idea of evil, the Force, as a metaphor for Protestant fears?*

GD: That is part of the Protestant dilemma in the North. I keep on saying the North but it's not the North I mean, because I only *know* Belfast. But there is the fear there's somebody out there, some kind of foe or enemy. And yet it can never really be defined. Politically it can be defined, but even Republicanism or Nationalism are big empty phrases, you have to be able to put detailed meaning into them. The particular guy in 'Speedboats, 1972', I remember quite well—by day he was a nice fellow and we could talk to him, but by night he became slightly weird, because he literally went over-the-top. And I just felt what a waste. He did see some kind of enemy 'out there'; but we could look out the same window and see nothing.

NMG: *'The Mainland' suggests longing: 'looking out somewhere over there/to the sea'. It seems to be a very middle-class Protestant image. Do you sense there is a religious sense of the Other, that unity with Britain is as ephemeral as a religious notion, such as Heaven?*

GD: I always wanted to write one poem, wanted to put on record the life that other people live; this kind of Protestant middle class life. It's not that I'm writing from, or *want* to write from, a unionist viewpoint. But I wanted to address those experiences. I was in a particular house and I saw these photographs, wedding photos and so on, and I thought this is a life that hasn't been written about. It kept at me, until I wrote that poem. It's actually about the loss of self, about the way in which these people have a right to be inarticulate. They *don't* have to talk to anybody, they can just be themselves. And I also wanted to capture the customs of their lives, that there is a certain essential vacuity there which I find deeply troubling. There is a very rich and dynamic Protestant culture, in so far as it's there in music and so on. But I'd like to take it out of the terms of it being a *political* culture and talk about it in terms of being seen as *only* a literary culture and a way of life. In many ways it's no different from Catholic culture, either. I think too many people are over-stressing the differences. If you take Belfast, there was a dynamic culture in the Sixties and early Seventies, which was squeezed by the Troubles. Now that was a common culture: it was music, it was dance, it was reading, it was very vibrant, fashion and so on. And I think that that almost led towards the democratic basis of a solution. But it was snuffed out. And maybe I could stretch it to say that I'm writing an elegy for that time in the hope that it'll come gain; but I'm not being nostalgic. Too much has happened in-between times.

NMG: *And in the present hiatus movement toward a similar balance hangs by a thread again? In 'Local People' are you suggesting that the three sections show that people are the same in NI, GB and Eire; yet the sectarian divisions continue here, although the same people can get on okay together elsewhere?*

GD: That triptych tries to link together different worlds using the language the people themselves are using, in those three different regions. And also to move towards, maybe not satiric but in an ironic way, the conclusion, which is a kind of a Biblical cry. I wanted to use the language of evangelical Protestantism. I remember I read that poem in Sydney, Australia, and a few guys who thought I was calling for some kind of apocalypse (which is far from the case) nearly chewed me alive! They misheard, misinterpreted—that's one of the risks you run when you go public with your work.

NMG: *In 'Likelihood of Snow' Northern Irish people are said to have "kept/to themselves in desperate innocence"; that poem was written in Canberra. Do you see the increasing cultural diversity as levelling barriers?*

GD: I was trying to get down my own attitudes to all these notions of identity. But also to make some kind of a marker in my life for what coming from Belfast means. And the people I grew up among, and so on. And placing this in a wider context. And that wider context was Canberra, the *planned* city. And in a way that's what so many political movements seek to do: to create their own place. And yet when it's done artificially, it ends up with this slightly empty place, which Canberra, forgive me, appears to be. The vibrancy has to come from people, and it has to develop organically, even if haphazardly.

NMG: *In 'The Water Table' you write: "I have seen the ground swell/and foundation cracks settle"—do you see this as an analogy for some other kind of settling down?*

GD: That was quite an important poem for me at the time that I wrote it, the mid-to-late-Eighties. At that stage I was beginning to go underground in terms of what I was doing. I've always been drawn to painters like Chagall, and Miro—lighter, you know, things take off. I'd not really written about the inspiration of visual art before. But I've always been drawn to those artists who throw things up in the air. So that poem is about the fluidity of life. And, importantly, that poem changed tack. My writing went in a different direction after writing that one. Away from *Lundys* and the early part of *Sunday School*.

NMG: *In 'One Summer' from* The Water Table *it's stated: "I left, what else could I do?" Is that connected to your earlier restlessness, a kind of nomadism, and the notion that sometimes the answer is to leave?*

GD: Sometimes it's the only thing that you can do. I think the more people realize that you don't have to stay in the one situation; that you can actually move and come back, change; that sense of movement actually invigorates life.

NMG: *It's just an accident of fate where you were born, what you were born into?*

GD: Exactly. But also, there's the kind of political, cultural dead-weight that builds up in a society when people feel that if you do move you're contravening, you're transgressing something, whereas in fact if you move and do come back you're giving breath back into the place. And so often we see that as a violation, a transgression, betrayal—and so much that's negative flows from that.

NMG: *And so that's why you quote Yeats' "water is the generated soul"—it suggests the collective unconscious?*

GD: Yes.

NMG: *In 'The Sticks' does the reference to family imply a source of peace of mind? Like the countryside, is it a solace?*

GD: I call it 'The Sticks' because I actually had in the back of my mind 's-t-y-x', which is another kind of crossing. And also there's the patronizing attitude a lot of people have to the country you know, the provinces and so on. But Ireland is a province: an island of provinces. It's just nonsense talking about the sense of a centre and periphery in a country the size of Ireland. I've always seen family as being an important thing in my life because I grew up with a family of women and there was a lot discussed at home, home as an important place where you could trust people. Now, regrettably, the last few decades have seen that sense of family, of home, exploded, because of so much damage that's happening to relationships within the family and around it. I'm not traditionalist in that I think the nuclear family's the only unit for society, far from it, but I do feel in my own life my wife and children and extended family are very important. And I write knowing that they're there; it's a stabilizing factor.

NMG: *In* Sunday School, *clearly the title captures the whole sense of 'Sunday' as a special, sacred time and 'School' of learning while you are young to fit into a particular cultural scene?*

GD: Yes, though in terms of the landscape there's slightly more of an ironic quality. Irony doesn't go down too well in Ireland, we're not too tuned in to irony, and we maybe take ourselves a bit too seriously. I have that ironic, sceptical vein in mind. Also, an important influence has been visiting Crete in recent years. I began to get involved with rescheduling the surface water around our home in the Galway countryside, moving it around and so on, and when I was in Crete I was thinking about the island surrounded by water. About the way water gives us life; but also when it moves up from ground water into a swell it could actually take the house up. The house becomes the island. And then you start to feed back into all the extraordinary mythologies. So *Heart of Hearts* moved into Crete. Without water we don't survive; the brain floats in water; the womb, the sea and the coast... all these notions. I always love the sense of a kind of a tremor in a poem, a surge, the way you have an after-effect. I love the notion of a poem having an after-shock. The more echoes it has the better. So that people can return to the same poem and it still offers something new to savour, it's not just over in one reading. I'm just fascinated by the way in which each word can carry inside it its own microclimate. And people can try and get those angles right. Just to get the word right, to get the angles on it right, so that it can catch all that light.

In the Chair

with John Brown

JB: *Born in 1952 you grew up in Belfast. "What our family 'means' and how we gather all such 'things' into our 'selves'?" is a question you ask of the poet Thomas Kinsella (*Against Piety, *1995). How would you answer this question about yourself?*

GD: I think it was an important part of my background that I grew up in a house full of women. My mother and father separated when I was quite young; I moved with my mother and sister from Downview to my grandmother's house in Skegoneill so I grew up there in north Belfast. My grandmother, who had separated from her husband in Canada and returned to Belfast to work in a well-known Jewish retail shop, Goorwiches in Royal Avenue, gave piano and elocution lessons from the house. She had a public life as a light opera singer so I was often referred to as Ethel Chartres' grandson. My mother, a more intensely private woman than my grandmother, stayed at home to run the house, only going to work in retail shops in town and, later on, in the civil service when I was in my early teens. It was a fairly typical lower middle class family with a fair share of tenacity and vulnerability and, I see now, an intriguing mask of being only these things. I was often unwell with asthma as a young boy but these women looked after me.

Off school periodically I'd read alone at the top of the quiet house with just the clock ticking—all the women of the house out and my sister at school. I recall reading dictionaries and magazines on films, which my mother, a great cinemagoer, would collect. I grew up very much on my own in those early days, but the house alternated between tranquillity and calm and a very dynamic family life: my grandmother, as an out-going woman, had friends around for parties or piano recitals; London relatives visited periodically; when my uncle was demobbed from the RAF he would bring his mates and girlfriends around so there was also this whole new dynamic of animated discussions and good-natured arguments.

We lived in a terrace of seven houses—a self-contained little canton of Protestants and Catholics with a surrounding immigrant Jewish community, a lower middle class world of small shopkeepers, senior clerks and widowers. Originally my great grandfather's people had come from Huguenot France; my great grandmother's people came, we suspect, from central Europe and who had married in Belfast early on in the twentieth century. My grandmother was very friendly with the Jewish community and one of my best friends as a youngster was a Jewish boy. As a boy you knew the territory between home and primary school like the back of your hand. There was a seasonal rhythm with "marbles", conkers and the yearly holiday in Bangor or Portrush (which seemed more *risqué*). During the July fortnight we took a house in Bangor and my grandmother's friends, like the stunningly handsome Annie Orr, would visit. Annie would recount stories of the B-Specials shooting up a family on the Cliftonville Road; she showed me the Catholic Nationalist experience of Belfast. Later you bussed across town to secondary school in East Belfast and a whole new geography with its own rhythms opened up.

JB: *How would you describe your early childhood awareness of that first environment though—the language or speech of home and the Belfast streets?*

GD: There was the way people spoke "proper" English through Belfast accents, a kind of Empire English that was slightly embarrassing and intriguing. On Wednesday afternoons when my grandmother gave elocution lessons, which were popular, you would hear the girls and boys reciting poems in that kind of accent. The feeling that the way we spoke was somehow inadequate and that there was a "proper" way to speak intrigued me. I remember visiting my extended family, in the late fifties and early sixties, who had moved to London between the wars, and being asked by a great aunt to stand up and say certain words like "mirror" and "film" in my Belfast accent. The request came from affection—not from an urge to humiliate or embarrass—from a sense that the way we spoke was somehow authentic. If you were mindful of the English spoken on the street and the extraordinary language the girls would use on the bus travelling across town, (an incantatory, half-mocking language which ended with them shouting each others' names like *"Jean-ne-o"*), there was also the language that you were supposed to aspire to (a type of tortured 'Cherryvalley' English); between these two there was the language of the place itself with its own phrases, words and terms—a Pandora's box, a treasure trove—and you discover that it is not totally understood everywhere (when you travel) and you become conscious of it (when you write poetry) later on. Every family has its own codes, its language, but there was a symmetry or fluency between the language of the house, the street and the Belfast buses and that is a tremendous resource for any writer to have. I've always been bothered, though, when a writer's sense of the vernacular or the idiomatic or demotic becomes too *self-conscious* so that it becomes exotic, an interest in itself, turning language into a zoo; an easy joke or expression of sentimentality.

JB: *Poems like 'Innocence' and 'Safe Houses' (Sunday School) have different perspectives on the second World War; 'Child of the Empire (Heart of Hearts) dreams up Churchill; there is your primary school headmaster with a spitfire in* The Rest is History. *World War II was important?*

GD: The second World War influenced everything from the clothes men and women wore to the style of their moustaches through to the attitude to cooking (if things were not quite hoarded, you still did not throw food out) and it influenced the physical environment in memorials and pre-fabs, which I can still recall, on the Shore Road, where people had been moved after losing their homes in the Belfast Blitz in 1941. This was only fifteen years later after all; there were still ration books and blackout blinds in the house. Then there was the whole military sense of the Empire in annual parades—Remembrance Day and V-Day—and the flags in the churches, represented the various battalions. In the history taught at school the second war was an all-pervasive background and, indirectly, it suffused the metaphorical backdrop of the films my generation watched where the great English actors, the Attenboroughs or John Mills, appeared. The political background was largely not taught but I remember Churchill's televised *History of the World* with Richard Burton's voice-over. The second war was our world and, in some senses, it had never really ended. You would see war veterans on the buses (with their navy blazers and regimental insignia badges); there were those damaged war-veterans who could not adjust to civilian life; some of the neighbours in North Belfast were Jewish or refugees; our next door neighbour had fought in the war and met his wife in Vienna and my grandmother had worked in an ammunitions factory. The war crossed divisions; it affected the whole tapestry of civic life in Belfast. The people who were honoured, or who we thought we *should* honour, or who we were told to honour, were all connected with the war. From Camp coffee in the cupboards to our awareness of battles in Holland or north Africa, there was the sense of Imperial connectedness, the sense that in some way we were all part of the one story.

JB: *The war penetrated consciousness that deeply? What about popular literature?*
GD: Yes. On Fridays you had a series of magazines or comics like *The Tiger* where the Germans snapped out instructions and there was always a good Tommy, a Scottish soldier or a Ghurkha. Christmas bumper editions, annuals, covered the story of particular tanks or battalions. We lived near by the Capitol cinema on the Antrim Road; I remember my mother telling me, in my teens, about her seeing the Pathe News images of the concentration camps, people being ill at what they were seeing, indeed not believing it at first. So the full story did leak through. A friend, Ken, whose father had been a rear-gunner in the RAF was attacked by Messerschmitts and described his experiences— that lit up another world. There were war posters and, at one level, the entire imaginative life was lived around the Imperial armies, navys and airforces; there were the military tattoos, 'Army Days' when you'd visit camps and jump into tanks. The television was full of it as well. There was also the sense—built in behind all this but never really explicated—that the war was linked with the defence

of democracy and "our" whole way of life. There was a fad in constructing little Airfix aircraft that you built and arranged in the bay window on perspex stands. So there was this construction of your own little bit of the Empire in symbolic miniature in the front room. It was all one.

JB: *You went to Orangefield Boys' School in the 1960's; Van Morrison had been there in the 50's only to find "There was no school for people like me." You note Mahon's description of himself and Longley as "Protestant poets of an English educational system with an inherited duality of cultural reference" (Against Piety). Did the poetry or culture you encountered at school relate to the needs of your imagination or to the place you were from? Are these contradictory needs?*

GD: These senses of place and needs of the imagination are not necessarily the same; we were taught English literature, very English work, and I now feel that this was a good thing; only to have had confirmation of where and what you are, as a fourteen year old from North Belfast, would not necessarily have been that healthy. I was lucky to have good teachers at Orangefield, such as Dai Francis and Sam McCready. Part of the deal was that you read, learnt and stood up in class to recite chunks of English literature. I absorbed Chaucer, Keats, Milton, the Victorians and, of course, Shakespeare. Literature was this grounding in, and probing of, the great English writers, which gave some sense of the language and its structure, its material fabric. Later you heard sympathetic notes and echoes, outside the main English tradition (like Yeats' early poems or ballads or a classic poem like *The Lake Isle of Innisfree*) so you had a sense of contrariness—that this was different from the great English writers like Keats or Chaucer or Milton.

The real echo was reading the American poets in *The Faber Book of Modern Verse*, edited by Michael Roberts; their language seemed very different—entirely fresh; a contemporary kind of language—and that electrified me, as did Stewart Parker's school talk in the mid-sixties, on Sylvia Plath. Alongside these writers you read novels like D.H. Lawrence's *Sons and Lovers*, so you had the sense that you could write out of the ordinary, domestic suburban life that was mundane or the family orientated—this *could* be the subject for writing. I read a lot of fiction—particularly in translation in those Penguin Classics: Gide, Camus, Dostoyevsky...

JB: *Your reading of American poets like Lowell and Wallace Stevens instilled a sense of language as transparent, democratic? English literature by the back door?*

GD: For a writer it is all down to how you hear language and energise it in poems. You can hear the language of the street or the bus, or the looser, less formalized English of American poetry but you have to know how to convert this and transform it into formal structures. I'm sure Keats heard the language of the street and knew how to convert it into more operatic structures. Milton created muscular, very literary lines in his poems; it is surely not one thing against another, or vice-versa, but a fusion of these things, so that one energizes the other. Sometimes you can fall between the gaps when the street language lacks formal structures or the literary language of a poem lacks its own life or energy. To write just idiomatically and think it's a poem is pure fantasy; it's like the fad for jokes, which string 'bad words' together. Just as it's a mistake to purely situate yourself within a literary tradition and to do no more than that. You can have all the language in the world but it will not add up unless you have actually something to say.

JB: *Robert Lowell added up?*

GD: I read Robert Lowell in a hardback Faber edition in Bangor in 1968; the poems, which struck me, were in *For the Union Dead* and some in *Life Studies*. There was a sense of Lowell's anger and bitterness so that it felt as if these poems had come out of my immediate environment—a voice full of clarity, an unrepentantly modern voice, a voice with erudition without showing off. I picked up on the tone of voice even though a lot of the references went clean over my head. Lowell's poems were full of edginess and irony and that sounded not too far removed from the language of Belfast in fact.

JB: *You also read the French existentialists—Camus and Sartre—in Belfast and somehow that seems appropriate?*

GD: Camus was the easier writer to read; Sartre was much more demanding. In *Nausea* and *Roads to Freedom* you have this story of a man cutting his way through a heavily politicised, problematical landscape so those were novels that a sixteen or eighteen year old from Belfast could draw on. Camus was much more intimate and he meant more; there was Sartre's haughtiness which was partly class-based. And yet Sartre give an extraordinary weight to the intellectual life—life had this extraordinary *other* world within it which should not be decried; coming from a political climate such as "official" Belfast then was, where the intellect was frowned on and where everything was signed, sealed and delivered—so what was there to talk or *think* about?—that was refreshing. Camus told a story which was more intimate, closer to himself, and he converted these into austere and structured narratives in the essays; there's the powerful, theatrical essay, *The Myth of Sisyphus*; in *The Rebel*, you had this opening into a huge political world, invisible to us until then; there's the violence in *L'Estranger* but there is also a life lived in the sheer brightness of the sun, which is appealing when you are looking out of a Belfast window at the rain. Camus lived in French Algeria so there was the whole sub-textual level about which nation you identify with but I would not have picked up on that at the time. Strangely, since I wrote about reading these writers in *The Rest is History*, a number of people my age have related similar experiences, so maybe there was a season for these things in Belfast. The city had a youth culture, an intense club life going on at that time (and much in Camus also came from the similar circumstances in that house on the hill in Algeria, although the entirely different climate offers no parallels). So maybe, we identified with that energy in the writing; it has that helter-skelter, breezy, out-and-about energy which also existed in Belfast then. This energy and "freedom", particularly in the underground life of Belfast from the early fifties and mid-sixties, has not really been logged, so the dour, dark, drab image of the city predominates or else the fairly artificially constructed, lopsided one of more recent times. Certainly, in many ways, Camus was my hero.

JB: *You sought Michael Longley's advice about writing in the mid-1960's and met Padraic Fiacc (1973) whose selected poems,* Ruined Pages *(1994), you would later co-edit with Aodan Mac Poilin. You see Fiacc as having "bridged the link between poetry and violence" (*The Rest is history*) to produce "central indeed definitive, poetic statements on the northern conflict" (*How's the Poetry Going?*). *Surely these writers are poles apart in terms of poems and dealing with the north? There's Longley's construction and Fiacc's fragmentation.*

GD: A friend of mine, Gary Williamson, had a sister who was taught by Michael Longley, so I sent him some poems through her and he wrote back a marvellous letter, a real schooling, with a list of books to read; that was important. Fiacc had a sense of the modernist aesthetic; he had read and absorbed people like Beckett, so there was this edginess and fragmentation and disruption, the breaking down of formal English and its shapes. Longley, and Derek Mahon, both have composure and produce what was once, foolishly, called the "well-made poem". Surely all poems, to exist as poems, have to be "well-made"? Anyway, Fiacc made poems out of the landscape in which I was literally walking and that authorizing of the landscape was extremely important in the early 1970's. Reading his early poems, like 'By the Black Stream', which is about a Belfast man being caught in the half-light of the moon, floored me. There is also an extraordinary irony and sell-mockery in Fiacc. He deconstructs the whole notion of "the poet" and the pretentiousness that sometimes goes with that title. The integrity of his work, at that level, is unimpeachable; it is driven by a need to get the right form for the experience that lies behind the work. Michael Longley's work draws down the classical world and marries it with the kind of suburban world I had grown up in. So here were two writers virtually diametrically opposed in every way— although the modernist aesthetic in Fiacc is almost counterpoised by the security, stability and artistic mass you find in Longley.

JB: Against Piety *sums up the period between leaving school and university (1968-71) as "London, hanging out in Belfast.... applying for a job, as a cub reporter at my great-grandfather's editorial home, The Belfast Telegraph".* How's the Poetry Going? (1991) *describes it as a time when "our lives took on a new weird meaning, we began to live more recklessly with a perverse bravado". I have a sense that 'home" and 'homelessness' imbedded itself in Northern poetry then; did you write poems in this period?*

GD: I did write poems although they were absolutely impenetrable, a form of Theosophy you could make neither head nor tail of. I wrote one poem called 'I'm Through', the title taken from Sylvia Plath's 'Daddy' poem, and it was eventually published in *Sheltering Places* in 1978. 1 did not write many poems but I read an extraordinary amount. I do have a sense now of 1969 as the year in which the curtain fell. The recklessness and bravado existed amongst a group of us who went to dances or parties virtually every night. Up to 1969 we were spoiled for choice; there was the extraordinary riches of John Mayall's Bluesbreakers, and Cream and Fleetwood Mac visited Belfast. There was also a vibrant club and R & B scene. You could leave a girl home after a dance and walk for twenty minutes across town into any area up to 1968-69 but we kept on doing that into 1970, pretending that nothing was happening, and that was crazy. It was pure luck that no one was badly damaged; by 1972-73 all that stopped as Belfast became sectionalised. After I was threatened with being shot—I was simply a Protestant in the wrong place—the penny dropped; the bravado had to go. As Belfast became segmented, a desert town, it's possible to see 1969-70 as the last gasp of that decade's openness; after that it went toke. Something was taken away from us all, stolen by the violence.

Looking back at the early seventies I think we experienced a state of shock, akin to the trauma after a car crash, the world we had grown up had concealed this poison. Like some writers I felt then that you 'had to' respond by writing politically. This was *my* home, *my* place. Something needed to be done, or said. You might have tried to rationalise the situation and work out the anger and frustration, to create a space that was personal and self-sustaining as a rampart against all of this. I also tried to 'conscript' poetry to politically motivated writing. I realise now you cannot do that without allowing time or space for the experience to settle. Increasingly I've felt there were no "lessons" to be drawn from history; History (with a capital "H") was, if anything, an encumbrance— and certainly not some kind of rudder. Some writers looked to Eastern Europe (to Poland, Russia or Czechoslovakia) for historical parallels and poets such as Mandelstam, but there's a certain artificiality in the historical parallels; what happened in the north, in Belfast, was more intimate and on a smaller scale. If parallels existed at all then surely Spain, with its civil war and religious struggle, was closer? This was a time I was looking in the wrong direction for *political* solutions; I feel now, without fatalism, that what happened was bound to happen because the opportunity for change had already been lost and squandered in the sixties. The way things were run in the north had not been challenged early enough and so, for two and a half decades, we had the "troubles" out of which people adapted as best they could to the changed circumstances of their lives. What else could they do, the paramilitaries moved in and the civic space in Belfast was lost. Only now is that whole problem getting slowly sorted out.

People made choices to plant bombs and take lives; they made conscious decisions to do that, and they will have to live with their consciences for the rest of their lives. But the main responsibility for political failure rests with the old Unionist party and the sectarian nature of the society, while the pursuance of a military solution by the IRA was the only other major factor in keeping the situation going; we have had to pay for both. How could *any* poet weave a way through those two massive, self-excluding forces? I just don't think it was possible. Maybe there was a withdrawal by writers into their own spaces. From Belfast, you have Michael Longley re-imagining the whole thing through great classical texts like the *Iliad*; you have Mahon meditating on the whole notion of history; you have Fiacc, who I think is unique in this regard, actually challenging it in the structure of his verse. The whole scene was simply uncontrollable; writers should not feel responsible for that. There was the demand on writers to have a "take" on the situation, but most poets were not giving that, so the responses naturally varied; for poets it is primarily important to write poems that work and to that end it does not matter where the inspiration or subject matter comes from. I have always felt a little outside the whole "northern poetry" thing, probably because I went to college in Coleraine and then left the north in 1974. I wasn't part of the scene although I know some of the poets individually, as friends.

I suppose I've always been a bit cagey about being part of anything. I don't know why that should be. It hasn't helped really over the years.

JB: *You studied literature at the New University of Ulster at Coleraine between 1971-74 where you wrote two plays,* The Skull *(1973) and* The Pawnbroker *(1974). What were these plays about? Are dramatic forms essential different from those required in poetry?*

GD: I published some poems in *The Irish Press* and which were read on BBC radio, so I was asked by the Irish Language Society in college to write a play, which would be translated into Irish. The first, *The Skull*, was about a speaking skull sitting on a rock becoming excited by the presence of women. The idea was lifted from Robin Flower's *The Irish Tradition*; the play travelled down to

An Damer, the Irish-speaking theatre in St.Stephen's Green in Dublin, for a season of one act plays, and then it was sent to The Gate, but I never got the script back from Hilton Edwards, though he was keen I remember to produce it, but the play's details are vague. *The Pawnbroker*, the second play, was a verse drama, a mix and match of priest and Orangeman but these were two under-graduate plays; I now teach theatre so I know the kinds of things needed to write well for the theatre and it's a different discipline than poetry. I don't think you can just "write a play". You really need to know what you're doing and why.

JB: *In Coleraine you joined the Labour Club, helped to set up the James Larkin Defence Committee and played in a band, 'Fir Uladh', at anti-internment gigs; a poem like 'Speedboats, 1972' indicates little sympathy for the north's middle classes. Does class consciousness register in your poetry? A loosely left wing position might be inferred from reading many northern poets; there's MacNeice's generalized sympathy for the left and Longley's sympathy for artisans.*

GD: I was very much on the left. I read Trotsky and Marx in the hope of getting away from the cramped politics of the complacent Unionist position on the one side and the very heavily authoritarian position of Catholic nationalism on the other. The hope was that socialism might create an effective wedge to drive change through. Coleraine drew a mix of students and lecturers from Scotland, the Republic of Ireland and England; Walter Allen taught there and he had been part of that thirties generation of writers, which had included Louis MacNeice. Allen was *very* influential at Coleraine when I was there. He introduced American and Russian literature and was a great teacher. If the teaching staff was generally on the left, the student bodies, with Scottish influence in the Labour Clubs was totally permeated by left wing radicalism. As students we would go to Derry to sell newspapers or mount protests against internment, that quick fix which energized opposition in the 1970's in the same way that Thatcher's treatment of the Hunger Strikes did in the 1980's. In the modern literary traditions of Scotland and the north of Ireland there has been a very strong left-wing influence; it seems to have congregated in bars and meeting rooms and parlours without really having an impact on northern power structures or government. You would have thought that

Queen's University might have been a cultural centre for the left but that was hardly the case; a writer like MacNeice would have been encountered at Queen's by pure fluke before Edna and Michael Longley repatriated him to the north. There was John Hewitt's egalitarianism, his respect for the political ideals of the left, his republicanism—he would probably have baulked at that description but the prose and poems are for an active contract between citizens and the state, which is a classic republican position. I imagine Hanna Bell, Roy McFadden, John Boyd—they would all be identified as left-wingers. Although it's not entirely visible in the cultural climate, the ether among writers was left wing; the tragedy was that this had never really been generally imbedded in the educational system so as to produce a generation in the 1970's who could effectively counter the sectarian environment. I have a great deal of respect for Hewitt's and Longley's artisans. I can see that virtues accrue from certain kinds of work. What really imaginatively interests me though is the way art is made or the ways in which you define a landscape through a mood or a shade or an angle of perception. 'Speedboats 1972' points up the complacency and acquiescence of the middle class in the north—in the same way that Hewitt did in his marvellous poem *The Coasters*—but I hope I'm not just taking an easy swipe because there are also virtues in that class; they helped to create stability while being deeply uneasy with culture. These things are never simple.

JB: *The north—west "triangle" (Portrush, Portstewart, Coleraine,) has inspired northern poems by Simmons, McFadden and Mahon. Does it surface in your work?*

GD: I've always been drawn to coasts. I grew up within sight, sound and smell of Belfast Lough. I don't think I consciously wrote out of the geographical scene of the Triangle although one or two poems set there appear in *Sheltering Places*, and this landscape often merges with poems written later or set in and around Galway. I think of Portstewart or Portrush now as signifying the staunchness and steadfastness of Ulster Protestantism; it's a landscape on the edge of things, both bracing and abrasive.

JB: Against Piety *and* How's the Poetry Going? *record the "importance" of Derek Mahon's work "Is there a poet of the 1990's for whom one will wait as one did in the 1970's for Derek Mahon's* Lives *or* The Snow Party?*" you ask. What is it in Mahon's work you relate to?*

GD: Mahon brought together different elements into the one imaginative frame; a modern contemporary idiom; the self-dramatising, self-ironising voice; the link with European writing and writers like Beckett, which I found attractive, and the anonymous, austere, remote, controlled shape of the poem. He creates these poems of extraordinary lightness and depth—there is certain chilliness and the more recent work is analytical. There is an imaginative weight in his work.

JB: *Moving to Galway in 1974 to research William Carleton you lectured there until 1987 while commuting "through those complicated and sometimes deadly chambers that divide one part of this island from another."* (False Faces, 1994). *The west has often magnetized poets. Yeats, WR Rodgers, MacNeice, Longley, Norman Dugdale. How does it register in your work?*

GD: I had been to west in 1973, but I moved down in 1974 after working for a brief spell as a librarian in the Central Library in Belfast. I really grew up in Galway as the pressures in the north of the early seventies that I carried inside me began to unwind. Galway provided a contrast I needed to discover; I'd been stung to the quick by what had happened in Belfast. Living in the west of Ireland I began to find that there were other Irelands—not just physically but culturally and psychologically. *Sheltering Places* comes from the initial awe I felt as a young fellow of twenty-two moving into an 'awesome', even denatured, landscape. As I started to live in a place where I would work for twenty years, I began to see through the landscape to the people and to the more domestic customs of the place. I wrote all of *Lundys Letter* from the west; there are quite a few poems about the west in *Sunday School* and *Heart of Hearts*. Between *Sheltering Places* in 1978 and *The Lundys Letter* in 1985 I started to re-imagine the Belfast Protestant background I had grown up in and wonder about my own family's diverse provincial and 'refugee' roots. As I was trying to understand my life in Galway I was—ironically and simultaneously—discovering my own background in Belfast and what these terms mean—"background", "Belfast", "my own".

JB: Sheltering Places *has that key image of a storm, which threatens shelter in the title poem, which makes it look, very much, like a Belfast poem. Are there also tensions between literary/historical traditions and the subjective "now"—"the passion that cries out of the ordinary" in this your first volume?*

GD: I wrote the title poem, 'Sheltering Places', in 1970-71 when I lived for a brief period in Ballybeen in East Belfast; it's not a west of Ireland poem. The hills in that poem are the Craigantlet Hills behind the estate and the storm clouds are literal as much as they refer to the 'troubles', which threaten to eclipse the ordinary lives of people.

On the whole though that book is emotionally stunned; a big influence and probably too strong a presence was Padraic Fiacc. I was trying to find a language that was non-'poetic', so Fiacc's voice was important and the poems are responses of which I was not entirely in control. I was trying to create a voice and to understand the literary tradition; I think there's a more realised voice in *The Lundys Letter*, which came after I had read more poetry and absorbed it into my own voice.

JB: Sheltering Places *alternates between a bleak western, almost existential, landscape (rocky, stony, rainy and empty) and Belfast's "poisoned... sloblands" where a river is "a haemorrhaged vein ", there is also the traveller in 'Seanchai' with "baseball boots" and "an inarticulate/mythology that/has no place/to celebrate." Your essay on John Hewitt and the poems set in Europe (with the moth as travelling "muse" in a suitcase) might be taken as indicating that outward horizons, not inward roots, are more important in your poetry? It also raises that old juncture between home and exile in Irish poetry.*

GD: I think you are like a metronome early on. You move between the need to place yourself, to put down roots and stabilise artistic foundations, and yet you cannot just remain on that ground; that tension lies behind many of the poems. At some level I have always felt 'rootless'. Maybe it's a genetic throwback! I need horizons and the sense of space to oxygenise or aerate roots, to avoid the work collapsing inside itself. It's not that travel particularly interests me; I like observing the "otherness" of other places. I've carried Belfast with me but I have *chosen* where and when I've moved, so I can't help but feel that there's often sentimentality in much of the talk around the notion of 'exile'. A man from Achill who had to leave for work in New York or Boston or London in the nineteen forties or fifties, would find this 'exile' had an entirely different resonance. These days though, with many Irish kids jetting back and forth between Ireland and the States, the whole notion of Irish exile has more to do with American perceptions of Ireland, rooted in the past, than with contemporary realities. If you are from Kosovo, say, exile has a very real and current meaning.

JB: *You edited* The New Younger Irish Poets *(1991) which includes northern poets who "grew up in the poetically charged literary environment of the 1980's" with their "unpretentious confidence... self-deprecating wit" and "keen tactics of evasion". Is there such a thing as "northern poetry"? Were the tactics of 1980's northern poets different from those of the 1960's?*

GD: Take it chronologically. There was a big breakthrough with the sixties generation—Heaney, Longley, Mahon and Simmons—who all wrote poems of the first order. Earlier poets like John Montague and Padraic Fiacc, a little before him, had fed into sixties writing but the younger poets wrote poems which achieved an extraordinary degree of world recognition, unthinkable up to that point. The second generation—Medbh McGuckian, Paul Muldoon, Ciaran Carson and Frank Ormsby—could 'call down' that achievement and play with it. Certainly Paul Muldoon has many self-ironising strategies and he can turn the tradition, to lightly make fun of it, but he's also sustained by it, and is, partly, its amanuensis. More recent writers, like John Hughes, have moved through Muldoon playfulness while avoiding the more magisterial sense of poetry. Critics, though, prefer groups to individuals; in that first movement of northern writers, so floodlit by history, you have writers who are so very different that, with hindsight, it's possible to see the *differences* as more defining than what they have in common as poets from "the north". The differences between Muldoon and Mahon are enormous; very little links Mahon and Heaney. Mahon might be linked with Beckett but where does that leave "the north"? To simply force these writers into categories under the auspices of "*northern* poetry" is fundamentally limiting; their differences have as much to do with specific cultural or religious experiences, as they have to do with anything called "The North" with a capital "T" and "N".

JB: Across a Roaring Hill *(1985), which you edited with Edna Longley looks at the religious factor; it is not a "sectarian sociology of art" but a reflection on the distinction between Protestant and Catholic, only one, albeit major, part of Irish experience...[that] has determined so much of what I am".* How's the Poetry Going?) *How do different religious backgrounds register differently in the style, language or subject matter of poetry in Ireland and in your work in particular?*

GD: I'll talk within a strictly literary axis. I think that people from a Protestant background have a different imaginative make-up from those of a Catholic background although there are crossovers and differences within Protestantism—the Church of Ireland and Methodism, for instance—because there has been a different schooling and cultural formation and this can produce different echoes in the writing. The mass and iconography, the sacred notion of the altar and 'serving' it, is fundamentally different from the more chaste emblematic furniture and austerity of language that defines Protestant churches. I'm not just talking about spirituality or mystery; the ways in which Protestants are called upon to honour the 'after-world' is entirely different. There is no incense and colour is so shocking because it's use is so limited; this means that every phrase or nuance carries a rigorous kind of significance. I went to the Church of Ireland on the Antrim Road as a boy and it inhabited a middle distance between Catholicism and Presbyterianism. Early on I was struck by the purity of language in the hymns, the iconography of the Empire in the flags; Old Testament stories and New Testament parables. There was also a sense of individual, even civic, responsibilities or morality that you could not just dump outside and leave at the church door. Some Bible stories, like the one about Jericho, surface in the poems as little cartoons. I'm not particularly interested, though, in either hitting the church or exploring its ministry or environment; I've not been scarred by this formation within cultural Protestantism to either want to do that or to fake a Catholic "Irish" sense of what I'm doing as a writer. There is the fascinating encounters between the renegade Joyce and Beckett in Paris; one tries to pull the entire world into the book and the other to flush it all away. Yet you still hear the whispered echo of the Church of Ireland hymnal or vespers— "Now the day is over, night is drawing nigh"—in Beckett's *Krapp*. In Beckett that takes on a shocking poetic charge; sung in church it can sound just like another cliché. I think that chasteness, that austerity of language is one inheritance of Protestantism for which I am thankful.

JB: *Your first three poetry volumes between 1985 and 1991 share, with Tom Paulin, the Belfast-Protestant background and landscape: clocks, mission huts, Orange Halls, terraced streets, the poet questioning recent Unionist history (Edward Carson and Covenants), "bibles and ledgers", living rooms crowded with knick-knacks. The language, narrative strategies and ways in which history is refracted through poetry seem radically different though?*

GD: How conscious this focus is in the writing of the poems I'm not sure but when I wrote 'Secrets' in *The Lundys Letter*, I felt I had got inside a world I had not read about, the type of domestic interior I had encountered in friends' houses which opened out into the wider civic landscape of Belfast. Initially I felt that this world had not been registered in literature although, re-reading Mahon, I came to realise that he often echoed this world and, in many cases, had been there before me. It took me ages to get a poem like 'Little Palaces' right, to try to capture that sense of decorum and of 'everything in its place'. No doubt there's a kind of psycho-babble that could easily caricature the rituals and routines of this Protestant way of life—painted kerb stones, wound clocks, mission huts and Boy Scouts—as defence mechanisms in a consciousness that is either unfulfilled or which has not engaged sufficiently with any other-world, or other 'side'. I dare say the same analysis might be made in regards to Catholicism. Primarily the poems you mention register a world, indeed, a 'civilisation', which was changing and has by now effectively gone. I thought it was important to register the integrity of the life in those streets, rather than to stand outside and mock it. That's a tricky line to walk. Some people have read these poems as authorizing a narrow worldview, but there is a critical stance, I think, critical, ironic, yet also understanding. I see the poet's role as primarily bearing witness—although that sounds a bit grand—and the excitement in the writing came from the attempt to get the visual imagery and metaphors right. I was trying, in those poems, to record what I saw and recreate what I imagined, in much the same way as a painter might; if there's commentary it comes out of that visualisation and the way we see what we see.

JB: *Do poems ever come out of the radio or televison? The sound of the radio sometimes penetrates the work of Ulster poets born in the forties; regional television came in the fifties as you have pointed out.*

GD: Radio and television often stand in for codes of passivity by which the world comes into the poems, so there is the sound of the radio or the flickering television screen in some of the poems in *Sunday School*. I'm not really that interested in furniture or easy statements of modernity—the "pylon thing"—and some critics have wanted more of the contemporary world in my poems. Television, radio, these kind of things are not that relevant unless as a backdrop.

JB: *You acknowledge Seamus Deane's critical writing in the seventies as an important influence on your own work; his* Strange Country, *though, looks at literature through the lens of history and politics (which are inescapable); your 1990's criticism surely tries to establish the imagination as having "priority" in seeking its own "freedom"?*

GD: I started off with the belief in the 1970's that literature should be deeply engaged with politics; I have now arrived at the view that politics can hamper or constrain the imagination. The books of essays in the 1990's attempt to see the value of poems—even where poems attempt transcendence or take politics on the wing— as poems, irrespective of what they are about. I'm interested in the poem—that stands on its own ground, so that its validity is not taken from the bigger picture. I'm interested in the poem, which defies politics and history, the poem that creates another voice, which is earned. There are some great political imaginations, particularly amongst novelists, but I'm primarily interested in the achievement of the poet when he or she moves into an imaginative world, which is both recorded and recreated, substantial and standing alone.

JB: *You commend, though, the 'passionate understanding of the political life of the imagination" of Bridget O 'Toole, and Derek Mahon's contention that, "A good poem is a paradigm of good politics—of people talking to each other with honest subtlety, at a profound level". Given that you "grew to despise the rhetoric of nationalism and unionism which no longer fitted into the realities of life in the Republic of Ireland or the Britain of the 1980's", is it possible to see the peace process, post the Good Friday Agreement, as a space where poet and politics might meet?*

GD: I think that poetry and politics should never meet under orders; I think they are in constitutional antipathy to each other. I'd paraphrase MacNeice in seeing the poet as a critical presence, challenging rather than conforming to political orthodoxies or communal beliefs. As a citizen in Ireland I have written critically about politics and cultural matters. I think, though, that there is no real middle ground between poetry and politics in the sense that poetry should be superintending the political world rather than the other way around.

JB: *The "troubles" though brought questions of national allegiance and writers' responsibilities; it's possible you might be read in the north as "the union's son turned republican" while in the south your critique of Field Day or nationalist culture as lacking "forms of inclusiveness" (Stewart Parker's phrase) was hardly sympathetic to an unexamined alliance between literature and nationalism. "What—ish my nation?". Has Joyce's Shakespearean question been superseded?*

GD: The whole notion of nationhood and those grand cultural categories have become less relevant because of the notion of fluidity and of 'opening up' now. I was walking down the street in Dun Laoghaire a few hours ago and there are now many Romanians and Nigerians and other emigrants and asylum seekers here. That's the world I now live in; the old rigidities of nation lead us into a thirty-year war in the north. It's much more interesting to find out the Englishness or Britishness of Ireland and the Irishness of Britain or the role of Scotland in the north-east without in any way losing the independence of these places as distinctive, self-governments. You only have a problem when people feel that by somehow engaging with these issues you are somehow diminishing what you were or are. Talk about "nation" is very cramped in Ireland and far too many critics and writers from other places like to treat "Ireland" as a special endearing case of and for nationalism. They're out of touch, most of them.

JB: *Why did you call your second volume of poems* The Lundys Letter *(1985)?*

GD: It was originally going to be called 'The Clock on a Wall of Farringdon Gardens, August 1971' after a poem included in that volume. The publisher, Peter Fallon at Gallery Press, was absolutely right when he suggested that anyone asking for that in a bookshop would hardly remember the full title. I came up with *The Lundys Letter* as an alternative. Even though Lundy is abominated within the Unionist tradition, as someone who turned traitor, I liked the notion of the transgressor and the historical backdrop. Surely the artist might be someone outside the camp who sends messages back?

JB: *'The Likelihood of Snow/The Danger of Fire' from* Sunday School *reads like an Australian/Irish poem; you visited Australia in 1987 and you have written about the poet Les Murray. Are there links'?*

GD: The connection with Les Murray is at a different level; in his poem 'Driving through Sawmills Towns' he gives imaginative life to a community most people would consider unsympathetically as being anti-art or against the imaginative life. He also wrote an essay on the way that the community he was from was viewed with disdain; I'd also witnessed that in terms of negative or simplistic caricatures of the Belfast Protestant side of my background. Les was exploring a world heretofore seen as distasteful. He was an empowering presence. I kept reading the work after I came back from Australia. 'The Likelihood of Snow/The Danger of Fire' is a letter back to the north, to my mother who was in Belfast, from the sunlit suburb of Canberra where my wife and family were staying. The 'fire' is the force of history which then seemed in danger of raising us all to the ground. It was the first poem where I actually started to talk about language and the way people use it to create identities for themselves as a community. Les also uses the vernacular in that way; he was important in that sense.

JB: *Your next volume,* Heart of Hearts *(1995), was described as "the most lyrical" of your volumes. How accurate is this word as applied to your work?*

GD: I would not consider myself to be a lyrical or musical writer although when I write I do read the work out so the sound of the line is important; it is the visual dimension of poetry, which fascinates me. It is not just the look of the poem on the page that is important— it's also the way you try to draw your reader in with the hope that they can actually physically *see* something. Some would consider poetry to be all *sound* so this idea would be anathema but it really does interest me. Perhaps the poems are lyrical in the sense that they are not big epic poems; they're generally small in their physical dimensions—if you blink they are gone—and I do put the demands of speech rhythm in poems, so that the reader can *hear* a voice directing them to what is seen. The sound of the voice 'saying' the poem matters most to me.

JB: *The three-line verse, between tightly buttoned couplet and quatrain, is a form you often use. Do you have ways of thinking about form, which recur in writing poems?*

GD: I tend to try to edit poems down even though I often have wanted to write big chunky poems but I generally know what a poem has to look like after living with it for a while. The Greek writer Yannis Ritsos who wrote chunky poems, which are almost sonnets, did fascinate me but, when I was starting out, I read Yeats' 'Cuchulainn Comforted' and became really fascinated with the three-line poem, *terza rima*, which he took from Dante's *Divine Comedy*. Passolini's 'Gramsci's Ashes' also takes that form. I tried my hand at it in 'A Fire in My Head'. Sometimes I've tried to draw something from Yeats for more solid poems such as 'Straws in the Wind', or earlier in 'The Proven Deed' or 'The Lundys Letter'. As I've developed I've come to see form as secondary to the tone of voice; that often tells you if you're casting the poem in the right shape. 'Sin' in *Heart of Hearts* was initially written as a big block but, as the tone seemed to reject the form, I opened the poem out into quatrains to sustain the voice. In that sense the voice or tone is primary for me in that it directs the form to its shape. There's no way I can be acerbic or self-mocking in quatrains, (they have too much composure without irony) but I'd use eight line stanzas to build up a head of steam, while couplets suggest you are going to spring. Some forms seem commodious, some withholding; trying to work out which will work best is part of the trick.

JB: *You have written about the jazz, r' n' b and traditional music scene in Belfast in the 1950's and 60's, the club scene from which Van Morrison's emerged, in* Heart of Hearts, *'Questions, Questions', with its repeated "you" and wisps of rhyme, remind me of a Leonard Cohen lyric; poems in* The Morning Train *(1999) sound musical. Do your poems assimilate the language or rhythms of particular music?*

GD: The connection between some of these poems and music is through the singer—not so much through the sound; there's voice in these poems singing. The voice matters very much. The pick up from jazz, R & B. or from people like Morrison is subtle, not conscious, but it's there like a refrain in a song.

JB: *You re-located from Galway to Dublin to lecture at Trinity College in 1988. Is there a Dublin perspective in the late 1980's and 1990's, which registers in the poems?*

GD: I moved to Dublin in 1988 and lived in college for a year before moving out to south County Dublin. Moving to Dun Laoghaire a few years later I had the extraordinary sense of returning home. South County Dublin has the feeling of an architectural and civic landscape akin to the north Belfast where I grew up in 1950's. I think this registers in some poems in *Sunday School*, like 'The Messages' which is set in Glenageary. At the time I wrote that volume, in the late 1980's, I was also reading John Cheever whose suburban landscapes—and his daughter's memoir, *Home before Dark*—seemed to chime with being here. I also discovered that it was very likely that my great grandfather's family—he was a Chartres—had lived in Dun Laoghaire and some of the family are buried in Monkstown -so there is that echo, although I'm not a great root-tracker and I view genealogies as fictions, at the best of times. After the family moved from Galway in 1992, I started to get more poems out of that relaxed feeling of living here. Dublin Bay is just below us and the mix of working class, middle and lower middle class houses and upper-class villas, registers in the poems in the same way, I hope, that a visual artist would draw these out of his or her ordinary surroundings, like the painters Utrillo or Dufy who I like a lot.

JB: *Visual art surely registers in your work: Marcel Duchamp's rages in 'A fire in My Head'; a woman's face in a bomb blast overlaps with Munch's 'The Scream', while Picasso, Magritte and Chagall enters* The Morning Train *(1999). You point out that Michael Longley looked to the Ulster painter Gerard Dillon and LS Lowry for inspiration while Van Gogh, Uccello and Dutch painting have inspired Mahon. In what way does visual art influence your poetry?*

GD: When I was at school I had a great teacher, David Craig, who taught History of Art and, at one stage, I even planned to go to Sussex University to study art history but I changed direction after school and stayed in the north. I'm no good at painting or sketching but I've always been fascinated by painting in particular. There's often that sense around painters or visual artists that what they do is physical work, which becomes art. I envy that. So much gets in the way of working as a poet; so much ego—fluff about "being a poet". I'm interested in images—as opposed to metaphor which can seem to be clever or artificial—and to get an image right seems honest, integral to a poem; it's also integral to a painter like Chagall who assembles the various diverse elements of ordinary life, in a little village, for instance, and then suddenly turns the world around or upside down. Even in Miro's abstractions you sense the physical playing with the canvas and an awareness of the perceiver. There is an intense relationship between the arrangement of the whole physical object and the structure of looking. I've always been interested in the way in which we see what we see and that has developed as a serious interest in *The Morning Train*. I once went to Magritte's house in Brussels; here was this very exciting, perception-changing artist who led a fairly standard bourgeois life, and you have a real sense, looking through the windows of his house, that he's still there. Painters intrigue me because I am fascinated by how we see what we see and many painters seem to have an honest unencumbered way of looking, so devoid of ego.

JB: *Do Irish poets now assimilate narratives from art whereas art used to assimilate or even illustrate literature in the past? Literature, perhaps, has lost a primary function or its number one position?*

GD: We live in a world drowned in visual imagery and bombarded with television advertising and electronic images: the MTV world. I sometimes wonder if the rigour and demand or the integrity and patience to read or hear a poem, is becoming a lost art in a world with quick fixes. Even the visual imaging of a popular song—the video—has become more important than the song. The superficial speed of a contemporary film or advertising seems to be more highly rated than the quiet interior reading of a poem that lays a depth charge. Perhaps things have changed so that the visual dimension of the poem, which was once highly rated, is on its way out because it lacks the expected 'speed' of the images of the MTV world.

JB: *Few Irish critics warm to Modernism or suggest that it has influenced Irish poetry. You note MacNeice's sympathy with Eliot's merger of street talk and the classics* (How's the Poetry Going?) *when you founded* Krino *in 1986 as a literary journal you named it after Ezra Pound's lexical gloss on the Greek word meaning "to pick out for oneself, to choose." Are these poets an under-explored influence in northern poets' work in general or your own work in particular?*

GD: It's embarrassing to talk about my own work in relation to an absolute master like Eliot. I've always been intrigued, though, by the way Eliot could move images around in 'The Waste Land' or 'Four Quartets'. There's an extraordinary stunning clarity and ambition in Pound. I'd never try to imitate this—I simply can't write that way—but I think that that kind of ambition lies behind Thomas Kinsella or, for that matter, Brian Coffey's *Death of Hector*, without ever being assimilated into the Irish poetic tradition. Eliot can locate a poem in a vast arena and then move in and out of different sounds and tones; similarly Coffey, in *Death of Hector*, breaks down the complacent solidities to give you a different read on the world as does Beckett. Perhaps I've tried to draw this world into some poems, like 'A Fire in my Head' while there's a kind of mishmash of Eliot and jazz beat in 'At Ron's Place', without going the whole hog. It's the tension between street talk, the classics and Beat that matters; creating a medium out of the differences: a living balance.

JB: *You edited* Yeats: the Poems, *a new selection (1991); your first poetry pamphlet had the Yeatsian title,* Blood and Moon *(1976). Surely Yeats' use of myth and heightened poetic rhetoric is a long way from the voice of your own work where even Joyce might encounter a U2 badge? Are you distrustful of myth or rhetoric?*

GD: I have a healthy disrespect for myth; I do not understand much of the information contained within it but I have a sense of its importance in Ireland and Europe. Having gone on holidays to Crete in the early 1980's I became fascinated by the labyrinth at Knossos; I started to read Ovid's *Metamorphoses* and see the maze as a template. *Heart of Hearts* emerges out of that "birthing"; the shape of that collection is very much determined by the shape of the maze. I also became interested in Minos the bull, the grotesque imagined creature in the labyrinth, and that became part of the opening poem, 'The Minos Hotel', in *The Morning Train*.

I'm interested in the gap or disjunction between the mythical past and the contemporary world; the way traces of a mythological membrane turn up in the present, through the eye of the imagination. The exact mechanism by which this happens I don't know; and I don't want to know.

JB: *In* The Morning Train, *the north seems largely to have disappeared as you travel into a landscape that is "neither here nor there" but still recognisably modern. The book seems full of questions. Are you optimistic or bleak about where this new century is going?*

GD: *The Morning Train* is a journey out of Ireland into Europe, carrying the freight of my own narrative and my own sense of discovery of what Europe is—the dark history as well as the light. I worked hard on the book's shape trying, constantly, to cross two things over in it: the sense of calmness, tranquillity and repose as well as the sense of the shadows from the past. I hope it's neither a bleak or optimistic book; I hope it's an artistic one. In the final poem, "Human Wishes", I'm trying to reconcile the entire volume and to understand through writing how things live and die and are made lasting by the imagination.

Twilight Zones

with Katrina Goldstone

KG: *When you were thinking about collecting your poems into* The Morning Train *had you set out to write about the Holocaust or did that just emerge organically as a sub theme?*

GD: A bit of both really. The core of the book *The Morning Train*, the chilly centre of it, is the poem based in Lodz in Poland, in the cemetery, the old Jewish cemetery. I was in Poland, giving a reading, and we were taken into the ghetto fields where the Jewish community had been killed. Just before the liberation, the Nazis took away many hundreds of Jews who were still alive in the ghetto. They dug six pits against the wall, they got the Jewish community to do that themselves, and these pits are still there. It's extraordinary to see them. Being in that cemetery and seeing those six pits had an extraordinary impact on me, it really had a very big impact and I wrote the little poem about that subsequent to being there. That was one thing that was happening in my mind, and in the poems. And then way back, in the early 1960s, when I was a young teenager I remember seeing in the *Observer* newspaper, a photograph, it must have been a commemoration or something like that. Anyway it was one of the famous photographs; I think it was in Warsaw, of a young boy being rounded up by the Gestapo, with his hands up and wearing a large cap, what we would have called a 'duncher' on his head. That also had a tremendous impact on me, that image, familiar at one level but frightening at another. And then the *Guardian* published a commemorative issue about Kristallnacht. It included a photograph of men walking, Jewish men, who were being rounded up. They were humiliated and shunned and if you look closely at the photograph, they are walking through a tree-lined avenue and you can see a woman smiling to the camera while behind her there are two other men looking rather bemused about what's happening. That was 1938 just a year before the whole thing blew up. Again the image stuck with me and I wrote about it in a sequence of poems called 'Europa'. So there was a merging group of images and things I had experienced and seen on the Continent over the last decade and I started to realise that in the book that I was writing. These individual poems kept on being drawn back towards a vortex and the vortex was the Holocaust. And then one other anecdote that links them together. In 'Europa' what I tried to do was to link together the experience of the 1930s with the experience of racial violence in the 1990s.

So there is a poem called 'Hero at Lansdowne', which is about a soccer hooligan—and again it's based on a photograph. This English guy is really freaked out at an Irish-English football match (it was abandoned because of crowd violence) and he looks as if he's in an opera [singing] but it's this perverse, un-locatable, irrational hatred etched on his face that struck me. It never seems to be far below the surface of our lives. So those kinds of passions are still there for this English lad, for what he calls the Irish. It seemed to me that this kind of irrationality and hatred was still around—just where it was being directed was different. The poem is a kind of warning, if you like. So all this stuff was in my head quite a bit. I was taking a train journey from Prague to Slovakia, up to the Hungarian border. The train was an overnight train and I was sleeping on the lower bunk near the wheels. I slept for about an hour, maybe two hours and woke up across the border when the guards called to check our passports. I couldn't get back to sleep and it must have been around three or four in the morning and I pulled back the blinds. It was still night. But as the train pulled into a station I could see this very long and (for me) unpronounceable name, of the local station we'd pulled in to, in the middle of

Slovakia. It occurred to me that there was something spooky about the journey and I couldn't quite understand why I was feeling so uncomfortable. I started to think of all those other journeys on other railways; it made me think of what had happened elsewhere. There was a link between those kinds of simple civic things, of traveling from one place to another on railway lines but yet there was, barely-fifty years before, these other train journeys, if not on those exact railway lines, on parallel lines. It was a strange, very physical sensation and I was glad to get to our destination and put the experience behind me. Around this time I was working on a poem called 'In Ron's Place' which is a poem set in a sunny hillside village in Italy, where I was getting over a bad bug that had laid me low. I was falling asleep in this place and then what I can only can call 'a blur' happened, being in that somewhat kind of twilight zone, from dozing in and out of sleep into being on the train and the way in which these kind of things merge under the surface of everyday life.

'In Ron's Place' moved in and out of these sensations, from sunlight to darkness, from domestic security to uprooted, uncertain, fear and suspicion. If you're European it's not as if you're carrying burdens all the time, there is this cultural subtext, or psychic subtext or psychic reality, which is there. So the train journey is one thing, simply a train journey. But then there is the not-so-long-ago history as well, of the trains with their human cargo, traversing the network of fifty years ago. I tried 'In Ron's Place' to link together the ordinary, everyday world of sunshine and life and relaxation and so on, with this dark side. The poem really became the bridge in the book between the two worlds, the contemporary and European and the darker history of the '30s and '40s. But I don't think I consciously wrote about the Holocaust with any deliberation or self-consciousness, it just came out. From a personal point of view there had always been a kind of affinity with the Jewish community, in so far as I grew up alongside the Jewish community in Belfast and one of my best chums was from that community. The interaction between my own family and the Jewish community goes back to my grandmother and my great grandmother. I suppose *The Morning Train* was the moment when all this just came out. It wasn't forced and it wasn't deliberate. It just happened that way. But I think it was only when I went into that cemetery and it had such an extraordinary, unforgettable effect on me, I felt I had experienced something that was an extraordinary moment in my life. [I do think] it is really shameful that Irish students are not exposed to this, that our obsession or preoccupation is with Irish history. The kind of theoretical knowledge of European history needs to be grounded in reality. It's not putting a trip on people that they *should* go but it surely should be part of a learning curve for young Irish kids so that they really understand what Europe's about, that it's not just the EU, economics, immigration, and such like.

KG: *Sadly I think that that's what a lot of them do think about. I don't think they realise about the darker side of European history because jobs, money, funding, our bright new identity is linked into that Europe.*

GD: In Poland I got a shock, an electric shock of recognition.

KG: *Because you can see the actuality of it. You can read all the books you want but until you're actually on the site of the atrocity its hard to comprehend.*

GD: And also the intimacy of the Jewish communities. That brings it right out because its immediacy, its individual distinctiveness and then you realise all that was just wiped out. Lost. It's unforgivable.

KG: *Well, if you take the example of the Listowel memorial [to the Holocaust], the way that came about was because somebody in the town had an interest in Primo Levi and the garden memorial was supposed to be dedicated to different artists in Europe but they separately set up a Holocaust section because one man was bowled over by the writings of Primo Levi and said this should be in here because this is also what the garden of Europe is about. It's amazing, that's there unacknowledged since 1995. Apart from publicity in* The Kerryman, *there's been little or nothing about it. They had a little ceremony with Mervyn Taylor and the Israeli ambassador and that was it. The point about all of this is that the man who was inspired to do this was inspired by literature. He wasn't taught it in school. Here it's in poetry where you find references to the Holocaust—in Michael Longley, Theo Dorgan, Micheal O'Siadhail...*

GD: I don't think it has really penetrated Irish poetry or writing spanning the previous generations. It certainly doesn't show up in any significant way in the generation of Patrick Kavanagh. Kinsella, yes; part of his 'Nightwalker', the line about the German 'brothers' who came over to Ireland to invest. That was published in 1968 and he also talks about it in some of his prose and lectures in the late 60s, early 70s

KG: *Some of the younger poets allude to it?*

GD: Cathal McCabe has written a long poem in the form of a letter, which takes in some of the themes we're talking about. I don't see it in any other Northern poet so significantly present as it is with Michael Longley. As in much else he has lit up areas of consciousness previously unseen or little regarded.

KG: *You're saying at one level, have I got this right, that part of this is not just an engagement with what Europe is. Underneath that there is a personal link, a personal response. Something is clicking in your head and that intersection of ideas and of the personal connectedness gives it another dimension.*

GD: It's the exposure not just on an intellectual level or an 'intelligence' of what happened [that I had] from my early teen years. Nothing could prepare you for the silence and the chilliness of being in such a cemetery, such a graveyard, nothing, nothing can prepare you for that.

KG: *It's that ghostly chill [you get it in the presence of ghosts].*

GD: Yes, a very awesome, awful experience but one you can't disconnect from other events. It's not just a simple matter of trains going throughout Europe, it's the connectedness of it all.

KG: *The irony of course is that originally Jews were travelling round Europe on other journeys. Those earlier journeys, not necessarily by train, represented mobility, and then others use that mobility as a means of your destruction. You can be brought from all corners, from Salonika, from France, from wherever, literally being transported to these factories of death.*

GD: The other thing about it, as you know in places like Munich, you can still see signposts for Dachau, it's not as if this is some ghastly 'other-world', it's close by—and so extraordinarily mundane the system that would allow this to happen. Michael Burleigh's book about the Third Reich, shows just how people, ordinary people like us, allowed it to happen. Some of them of course were actively supporting the Nazi regime, but others just saw it as a new way of life for themselves, and to hell with the 'collateral damage.' The 'collateral damage' effectively pitched European civilisation into the darkest night imaginable. I can't think in modern times of any other experience such as that. I know people say it's wrong to make comparisons but it's the sheer mechanism of it all. As a counter to that I suppose poetry is possibly the first and last way of maintaining the memory, of being the great minder of all that and I think that's true. I think of that notion of commemoration that's embedded in the whole notion of writing…in some way poetry is the only resource for people who have no immediate or direct experience, I mean family experience, personal experience [of the Holocaust]. There are certain risks of course. Think of Sylvia Plath who became unhealthily drawn to the theme. But if you look at the dignified orchestration of images in Michael Longley's work, in *Gorse Fires*, for instance, or *Ghost Orchid*, there is a selfless-ness in his writing, which takes it beyond the shocked and damaged engagement of Sylvia Plath.

KG: *And there are some echoes of these preoccupations and concerns in your new collection* Lake Geneva *too—migration, exile, poetic remembering, the husbanding out of memories, using memory as a bulwark against the present?*
GD: Yes, I revisited the upper north side of Belfast where I grew up and became annoyed at what had happened to the neighbourhood. It was stupid of me. I was angry too that after all the killing and pain that people have gone through during the 'Troubles', I couldn't see the 'gains'. The district was more divided than it had ever been. I felt like one of the old folk left behind, trying to live the lives they always had done but this time on an 'interface' between one side or the other; so some of the early poems in the book come out of that feeling. And the book takes off after that into other places, some of which have experienced bitter divisions, community strife, like Cyprus, for instance. In a way *Lake Geneva* is the closest I've come to making an artistic statement about what poets 'do'—with words, with the past that has been handed to them, with the lives they live, or try to live. You're right, though, 'memory' is the bulwark against the down side of our present, or memories turn into forms of resistance we call poems. I don't know. To use that great cliché, at the end of the day, you just write about what comes your way: sometimes it's fearful, sometimes delightful, and sometimes elusive.

The Poet's Chair
with Alan Titley

AT: *I'd like to talk to you at the beginning about your youth and upbringing, and what kind of a childhood you had, and how you spent it.*

GD: I grew up in Belfast in the 1950s in a mixed area, as they would say, insofar as that there was a significant Protestant and Catholic community, a significant Jewish community, and a smattering of different refugees and immigrants from the Second World War. So it was a rich community there. If you were thinking about it in class terms it would be lower middle-class, but the kind of housing moved from working-class houses to terraced villas to some significant, substantial villas on their own grounds. We used to, as kids, walk around. We spent a lot of time walking, and walking, and walking. There was a gang of us, about six or seven of us, and we kicked football, we had our surreptitious cigarettes down the back of alleyways. Everybody worked in that community, it was a very dynamic kind of community so that the men were gone during the day, and you had a sense of a routine and a ritual to the day. The bus was there on time, people were standing at the queues waiting to go into work. Belfast [city centre] was only about fifteen or twenty minutes away. It was a very traditional, stable society, but of course underneath all that, as we now know, there were a whole lot of undeclared tensions and things which were going to break out in that society.

AT: *Were you aware of that at the time, growing up?*

GD: Not really, because I was fortunate in that my mother and grandmother were very liberal, in the non-political sense of the word. I was kind of looked after by a Catholic family two doors up, it was like a foster situation whereby if my mother was out I would stay with this particular family. Some of my grandmother's peer group, her friends, was Catholic. Indeed, one of them I remember very much with great affection, Annie Orr was her name, she wanted me to be a priest, and I mean the thought of that! Anyway, I remember sitting on the sofa with her and her telling me I could have a great clerical future. Needless to say I didn't go down that route.

AT: *You've no regrets about that, do you?*

GD: Ah, I'm not so sure, no… I mean, I think that was a choice well made, not to go down there. But I mean, what she talked to me about was not just that sort of dreamy chatter, she also talked a lot about her experience growing up in Belfast in the 1920s, and that was an eye-opener. She lived close by on the Cliftonville Road, a famous incident where the B Specials shot up a Catholic family and I remember her telling me about that. I would have been, probably about ten or eleven and that lodged itself with me. And of course this was just ten minutes away from the stability and the coherence of the world [in which] I lived. So the troubled world was yet to come, but it was like a kind of a shadow underneath, and any time an issue came up, or any kind of quasi-sectarian [comment] my mother was quite strong-willed and she would have no truck with it. She was quite a brave woman, actually, now I think back.

AT: *Do you feel that that sort of upbringing, that your poetry is rooted in that sort of almost idyllic or cocooned growing up in any kind of way?*

GD: Yes I do, certainly a part of the early work comes from a sense of coming to consciousness about that world, as all writers do. It was a very 'intoxicated' life insofar as it was very routine to live as a young boy in this house with women, with my uncle returning from the RAF every so often. And to break out of that was a big act, which was what I did in my late teens. But looking back on it, there was music played. I have a very strong, almost hypnotized notion of the house. I can actually remember myself back into opening the front door, going through the vestibule door, and walking into the hallway, and there were three or four silhouettes, and I can actually see those. The silences of the house, the dark pools around the house, the furniture--I have a very tactile sense of that world. The view out the windows which was more or less, overlooking Belfast Lough. There was a sense in which the house became like a kind of a retreat or a refuge. But I think that's a myth; you have to actually fly the coop.

AT: *When you did that when you went to school, to high school, was that a development of something or was it a release? Was it an escape, or was it a broadening of horizons?*

GD: Belfast had a very strong sense of itself as being one city, and moving from north side across to the east where I went to school was not such a big wrench as people may consider it to be now. People used public transport a lot; you moved around the city a lot, people knew how to get off at one stop to pick up another bus going another route. There was that sense of a map, people moving around. But certainly, there's no doubt about it, when I went there [Orangefield Boys' School] when I was eleven, it was a wrench. It's not as if I was a spoiled brat, far from it, but I had a very stable and secure environment as a young boy. The friends I had had a similar kind of experience. So suddenly you were out and about, and of course I took to it with relish. There was a sense in which traveling across Belfast was actually not just traveling to somewhere else, in my case over to east Belfast, it was actually leaving something behind, and that was the first steps away [from home].

AT: *And when then did you have the first intimations that you might be a poet? Was that something that was always with you, or did it come with one blinding flash, or was it something that sort of crept up?*

GD: Well, it kind of crept up. I mean, it was a sort of secret that I kept for quite some time. Indeed, I remember only my friends, my really intimate friends, knew that I wrote poems. I used to write them in these school science jotters, you know where the graph...

AT: *Was this in high school?*

GD: In high school. So where you have graph [paper] on one side and ruled paper on the other. I was absolutely useless at science, so I used to spend the time doodling but also writing little bits of poems here and there. Then when I was about fifteen, a poem was published in an anthology. I can't quite remember the mechanics of why this happened, but it was announced at school assembly. And of course I was devastated, because to me this was a... it should not have been... no-one should have known about it. So I denied that it was me, I said it was another G. Dawe.

AT: *There are a lot of them around.*

GD: Exactly. I don't quite know why, but it was not something that you spoke a lot about, you just went on and did it. It was a sacred thing, you know?

AT: *Was that because it was a personal sacred thing, or because you felt that there was no respect for poetry or there wasn't a poetic tradition around you?*

GD: Well, in a sense, there was a poetic tradition around me, insofar as that my grandmother taught elocution in the house, and she taught piano and singing, and her anthologies were around the house, and I used to read these. I resisted, I think I only did two sessions with her on elocution and then I thought this was not for me. But the girls used to come in and the young boys used to come in and we would hear them learning how to actually talk 'properly'.

AT: *Were they trying to get rid of their Belfast accent?*

GD: Exactly, and rather than shipping them across to England to do that, they actually sent them to my adorable grandmother, Ethel. You could see the split that when they were in our front room they were speaking 'proper' English, but once they opened the door they were back to their own local accent. So there was a kind of sensitivity to language and to poetry in the house. My grandmother was a professional opera singer, and when she got too old she started to go into this other world of elocution and singing lessons. She used to have recitations and so on, so I could hear that in the background. But the sacred thing, what I'm saying is that it's an intensely private thing, so that if you wrote and published, as I ultimately did, that was one thing, but the idea was that you wouldn't go along marking it up.

AT: *Did the school syllabus help in anyway, the sort of poetry that you were studying in school, was that a source of inspiration, or something that was entirely foreign to your own sensibility?*

GD: Well, I think in a way it was both. Now that I'm much older, I mean, throughout that period of time [late 1960s-early 70s] I was always banging on about the notion that literature had to be 'relevant' to people. I actually think literature shouldn't be relevant; they should actually try and find it for themselves. That's a lesson that I learned at school, because what happened there was we all did our 'O' levels and our 'A' levels, and of course the syllabus then was stretched throughout the UK, Northern Ireland being a part of that jurisdiction. We were taught Chaucer and Keats and Shakespeare and so on, all the classic English writers, but one of the anthologies that we had to work from was the *Faber Book of Modern Verse*, edited by Michael Roberts, and subsequently new editions came out with Peter Porter or Donald Hall doing supplements. I still have my copy from 1966-67. In fact, it wasn't mine, it was a friend of mine at the time, and I obviously took it away with me, but it's been with me for those thirty years in between. This anthology blew my mind. The anthology introduced not only Gerard Manley Hopkins, and Yeats, and Wilfred Owen and the turn of the last century great writers, but there was Robert Lowell, and Sylvia Plath, John Berryman. Seamus Heaney ultimately would be brought in, Geoffrey Hill, Theodore Roethke. Particularly the American writers, the American poets; suddenly a door opened, and I can remember the exhilaration of that. Here were writers who were writing in an English which was different but was still English. It seemed to be closer to the kind of wry, ironic intensities of the world that I knew as a young man growing up, rather than the operatic English mode, which was there as well.

AT: *Apart from Seamus Heaney who you just mentioned, you said elsewhere that you didn't read Irish writers, didn't read Irish poets. When did that begin?*

GD: I went to University of Ulster at Coleraine, it was one of the first intakes for that college, and the writers who were on the kind of screen then were Kinsella and Montague, and Derek Mahon particularly, who was a writer in residence. They were the writers that we read, but the entrée [for me] into Irish writing probably came from my grandmother insofar as that she had a great fondness for Yeats. But Irish writing stopped at Yeats in my mind. Then when I went to college, a lot of my friends were 'into' the Irish language— speaking Irish, doing degrees in Irish writing, folklore and Irish language, and they opened the door on writers like Sean Ó Riordain, Mairtin Ó Cadhain, and so on. And suddenly you realize that there was one literature in Ireland with two languages, and that was a real charge, a real change of voltage, that here was something that you had no idea was there.

AT: *You had no suspicion of this before?*

GD: None whatsoever. It was never a part of my consciousness whatsoever. I mentioned the fact that two doors down from us, we were very close with a Catholic family. One of the girls in that family, if memory serves me right, was actually learning Irish, but it didn't seem to permeate our environment. The woman between us and her was an Austrian who was a refugee from the war, and we had more of an understanding of *her* dilemmas that we would have had of any others. But I think the thing about all that is, that was a revelation, and it was an excitement; it wasn't a burden. It happened in a random way. Alas, what it's now become is so heavily juiced-up politically, where as then people went into those realities in a more natural way.

AT: *When you began writing then, did you have a sense of yourself beginning to write as an Irish poet belonging to some part of that tradition, maybe adding to that tradition, maybe being on the edge of that tradition, or were you simply interested in writing your own poetry and it didn't matter where you fitted in the scheme of things?*

GD: It didn't matter where I fitted in. Basically I think that I was a poet that happened to come from Belfast. There was an anxiety early on, and it would be untrue to say that there wasn't, probably in my mid-twenties when I left the North and moved to the west of Ireland. I mean, half the reason why I decided to go there was because of the Gaeltacht and I wanted to actually learn Irish and really submerge myself in the culture in a way I hadn't done previously. That didn't work out for a whole series of different reasons, but probably around that middle twenties, middle to late twenties, I was anxious to define what this 'Irish Poet' business meant. But when I got that out of my system, I realized that trying to be so self-conscious, becoming conscious about being Irish is actually more of a hassle than just going out and writing your work and taking with you what you've come from and where you've come from. In my case, I started to realize that it was a very interesting cultural background which had been sort of closed down in many ways. I mean, I heard my grandmother telling a few stories, and my mother and so on, but I only later on discovered that my great-grandfather was from a Huguenot family; the woman he married was from, we think, somewhere in central Europe, her name was Quartz, and that there was a very intriguing kind of cultural mix in the background. So that started to draw my imagination much more so; it took over from any anxiety I had about, 'Was I an Irish poet', or 'a North of Ireland Poet'. I was described once as being 'The Belfast Poet from Galway', which was a nice triangulation, I mean, because they knew I'd lived so long in Galway, and yet here was this Belfast background so how do you link it together? Now I don't think people give a damn.

AT: *Have you modified that view over the years? That was, you said, in your early twenties you were anxious about this, and you've written a lot of poetry since, and we've all become more aware of traditions and what they mean or what they might not mean. Does that sort of still haunt you in any way, or have you just simply dumped it?*

GD: To be actually conscious of that all the time, that's gone, I think I've worked that out of my system. From time to time, when you're outside the country the question comes at you, 'How do you see yourself?' and people are unsatisfied, dissatisfied if you say 'I'm just a poet.' They don't really want to know you if you're 'just a poet'. They want to know you because you're an Irish poet or a 'this' poet or a 'that' poet. If you just say, 'I'm a poet who happens to come from Belfast' the eyes glaze over and they're on to something else, possibly understandably, I don't know. But I think that we've gone through all that. We've gone through all of that self-examination as a culture, and that the big issues are how do you relate to the world, how do you relate to Europe, how do we redefine our relationship with the 'Celtic' Diaspora and so on. All of that seems to be to me much more important than this constant interior dialogue that's gone on. I don't know what other people feel, but that's certainly my view.

AT: *Ok, but inevitably while you were growing up coming from Belfast going to University in Coleraine, and with the 'Troubles' starting and then in full flight, if that's the right word, which it isn't, and then you had other poets writing about this, maybe in oblique fashion, maybe not very direct, being cautious, but nonetheless you can discern sides or discern a point of view. Now what was your take on that? Did you decide to take any position as a poet on the Northern Ireland problems?*

GD: Not so much as a poet, I don't think I took any sides as a poet. But I certainly had a political engagement. I would've called myself in many ways a very committed Republican. I believed, and still believe, in the unification of the island. And I would have had a somewhat ambivalent attitude at a particular time to the armed struggle, which I no longer have or hold. But in terms of being a citizen, I had a very strong political position which has ameliorated over the years and I've become wiser. As a poet, I don't think so. It's so long ago now, we're talking thirty-odd years ago, but certainly there was a kind of irritation, there was a feeling of need that some kind of address had to be made to the issues around. I think the political commitment that I had then also knocked into that, and I felt that at some level if you're a poet you should be engaged critically with the society that you're living in.

AT: *Do you think that poetry can make a difference in a political situation?*

GD: Well, I'm not trying to work my way out of that, but it depends on the political situation. I think a poet like Pablo Neruda, his engagement with Chile certainly creates a different kind of voltage, a different kind of attitude. I'm not sure. I mean, in our context, you look back to the Thomas MacDonaghs and the Padraig Pearses, in many ways their poems are all about lamentation; they're about a kind of built-in sense of grief and a yearning for some transcendence. The generation of writers that I belong to, you can look throughout their entire work, both the poets and the playwrights and the novelists, and there's not that sense of looking for lamentation, it was too hot on their necks. I suppose the only value poetry has in that kind of social context or engaged context is that it gives a space for people who come from different kinds of backgrounds and indeed political ambitions to actually meet in a kind of neutral zone. I know that sounds corny, but I think that that's what the poem does, almost on the page.

AT: *Do you find that there's a tension, or a conflict even, between the personal and the public in your own poetry. I'm thinking of a poem like "The Interface" which is kind of an elegiac poem, a sad poem, and there may even be anger hiding, lurking somewhere in the middle of it, and yet most or a lot of your poetry is very personal. So I'm just wondering, do you feel that tension?*

GD: Well, I do, and I suppose if I have anything that defines my work such as it is, it's that I often see through private or personal detail a kind of public aftermath or a kind of a shadow of a public world. More than language, which is… we speak language privately, but at the same time it is a public possession, it's owned by others. I mean, most of our individual experiences have got that kind of public dimension to it. So in a way, if I was to try and render it as simply and directly as possible, for me the public world is rendered by the poem, it's revealed by the poem, but once you go looking for it, it becomes too obvious. Maybe a better way of putting that is that the poem for me is actually the way in which the public is revealed without losing contact with the personal.

AT: *When did you find your own voice as a poet? Do you think your work has developed from the first collection to the present time, and when were you happy that this was you, Gerry Dawe, speaking?*

GD: I've quite a clear line on that, because my first book came out in 1978, published by Blackstaff, and I was very proud of it and very pleased about it, but it really wasn't 'me'. It was somebody else who was trying to cope with a lot of interior disturbance about the society that he had grown up, had started to disintegrate, and who was almost unwilling to talk in the poems. So that came out in 1978, and then I didn't publish a book for another seven years, which is quite unusual for a poet in Ireland. In my case it was probably a good idea. In those seven years, my own voice started to come to me, and it was a voice which was in some senses Victorian, which was slightly mocking, which was also what I heard in the house, and it sort of took off then. So, the next book came out in

1985 and I felt that I had become 'me' in some strange way, and then the volumes started to appear much more [regularly]… not that I'm saying that's a good idea, but that's just the way it happened. When I look back at 1978, and those poems, which were written in the previous four or five years or more, [I wonder], "Who was that person?" Not to make too much out of it, I think I found my voice round about the early 1980s. And I even remember, I think, the moment when this became almost known to me. We were living in Ballindooley in Galway, and *Magill* magazine had just published a ten-year retrospective on the North, and in this there was a photograph of a famous incident which had taken place in Belfast, which was the burning of a street, Farringdon Gardens. In this photograph, the more I looked at it, you could *actually* see one of the old-fashioned clocks that people put on their mantelpiece was left on the wall of this house, and behind of course the houses were in ruin. As you looked closer at the clock, you could see it was at seven-thirty. So immediately it just went from looking at that photograph into a poem which starts, "I am the clock on the wall at Farringdon Gardens / I stopped dead at seven-thirty" and suddenly the clock was telling me the poem. And I think that was the key, the door into a community or a world which I had actually walked past. It was a world that I had known growing up… the mantelpiece clock was a symbol of industrial society. That's the clock that chimes in the morning, that's the clock that chimes at night, that's the one that's given as the gift when you retire, it's this sort of statement, it's almost an icon of industrial society. And when I saw it left in that random way, it seemed to me to be "this is the moment"--and I wasn't thinking this, but that's what was coming at me--"this is the traditional symbol, and this is what's happening to the world, behind it, these houses in ruin."

AT: *Of course, there's another sense in finding a voice, which is finding the language, and what strikes me is that you were speaking earlier about Shakespeare, and Milton, and Keats, and Chaucer, and their kind of wild presences in a way, they are overblown or overstated. Yours is very understated poetry, subtle and quiet in a sense. When did you discover that you had to write like this? Is that a deliberate choice?*

GD: It's deliberate insofar as I couldn't write any other way. When I've tried to write big, long lines like a Ginsberg, after a while I have to start cutting them back. I think there are two things at play there: one is that, I bring you back to those silhouettes. I grew up in a very [orderly world]... everything was in its place. So I have that sense that the poem has to look right on the page, and when I try and make it look otherwise, it's like combing my hair the wrong way; it goes against the grain.. That's the first thing. The second thing is that I mistrust eloquence, and I mistrust rhetoric of any kind. The poets that I've been reading more and more and more, in translation in many cases, like Montale, the Italian, and, Robert Lowell. What I love about their work is when they make you do the work as the reader, so you have to come into the poem. The poem isn't going to say, "this is what I do and this is what I am, amn't I nice? Isn't this an enjoyable experience?" It's more like art, visual art, or a piece of music, whereby you actually have to give yourself to it. Some critics have referred to my work as being sedate. I don't know about sedate. Shaping art, if that means what is sedate, well, I'm sedate. But I also like to inveigle into a poem a shock, and it needs the reader to be alert. So I suppose the eloquence and the rhetoric of the great English writers turned me off in some way.

AT: *Of course the great Irish writers as well...*

GD: Oh, and the great Irish writers, indeed.

AT: *It's a very 'un-Irish' thing to suspect rhetoric and eloquence.*

GD: Yes, I mean, my Yeats is the Yeats of country towns, it's the Yeats of small rivers, it's the Yeats of a very defined [world]... Once he goes down to Byzantium, I've walked away, you know. I find those poems just too highly charged, too expansive, if you like, too expensive for my taste. Whereas in "Nineteen Hundred and Nineteen", when he really has it marked in, there's nothing to beat that. My Joyce is the Joyce of *Dubliners*. Hopefully this doesn't mean that I'm a mean writer, but I hope it means I'm probably scrupulous! Some of the images in Joyce are spectacular. When Gretta's at the top of the stairs in "The Dead" and Gabriel looks up, he doesn't understand who she is for a moment, it just reveals so much without *saying* a thing. That's the kind of control and understanding that I'd like to bring into my poems.

AT: *So are you more suspicious of the traditional baggage of poetry than of metaphor and rhetoric? I think rhetoric is a good thing myself, but we disagree on...*

GD: Rhetoric is good if you know how to do it; I don't. I mistrust myself when I go down that road. I always feel that I'm hamming it up, or that I'm impersonating something else. I mean, some of the great Irish writers, or maybe I should put it another way, some of the great Irish writers that I respond to most, are anti-rhetorical, like Beckett. Beckett is the great writer of the anti-heroic, the anti-rhetorical. I don't know how far you can go down with that, though. I mean, it's a punishing, punishing road that he goes down. It's almost as if you'd like to try to marry two different codes, or two different modes. You think about the sort of anti-rhetoric of Beckett and the sort of unpredictability and naturalness of D. H. Lawrence. If you can marry those two.... If I can marry those two, I'm a happy boy.

AT: *You mentioned earlier Montale, and Lowell, and obviously poets that you like. I wanted to probe that a little further because I think every poet, they have their own favorites and the people that speak to them deep inside, not necessarily, obviously, in the Irish tradition. Who are yours? Who are the people you return to again and again, that give you inspiration, that give you sustenance?*

GD: The early books of Robert Lowell would be in my top five. Against what I've said, I think Yeats. My mother bought me, for my, I think it was, my 18th birthday the standard Macmillan Collected, and it's been with me through thick and thin. So the Yeats is essential. Unquestionably, of the Irish writers, there is just so much to select from. But I think of the slightly older generation, Derek Mahon would be a particular favorite of mine, in the way he domesticated imaginatively a landscape which I came to later, so I see the world a little bit through the way he has written it. I suppose Lowell and Mahon and Yeats. I wouldn't sit down and read Tennyson or Keats. I would sit down and read Blake. I think it's important for writers, for young writers, for people who are reading, to go against the grain, to go against what sits easy with them. And one of the problems of contemporary education I think, if that's not too haughty a way to put it, is that we have conceded too much to 'relevance', so that young students in secondary and third level *aren't* being exposed enough to difference, to the things that drive them daft: 'I can't stand reading Milton'! It's a very good healthy sign, because suddenly they're actually hearing Milton, and [grappling with] the architecture of his imagery; it is incredible; like going into another world. Rather, as if you say 'Okay darling you don't have to do Milton, let's go on to *blah-blah*, which is so much easier'. You've conceded too much ground. Literature shouldn't have to be complex or difficult. But I think when you actually discover a writer like Milton, you're into another planet.

AT: *I agree with you. I often think that you have to, if you love writers, there also has to be writers that you really hate. I think it's a great thing, a good hatred of literature, very healthy, and just to comment on that as you mentioned it, you're a university teacher yourself and you're deeply involved in creative writing, the creative writing process. Do you find that it is possible to teach? Do you find it useful and do you find your own prejudices coming to bear on the writers that you have in front of you?*

GD: If there's one thing that my upbringing gave to me, and I didn't realize this until much later on, was disinterestedness. Not for any political reason, but to take anything on its own grounds. Now I don't know why. I mean I have prejudices like everybody else. But, I always find that it's an exhilaration to work with young and not so young writers, when they're beginning to concentrate on their own and they have a particular time frame in which they're working. I don't really mind what [that work] is, as long as what it is, is the best it can be. And getting that structure in place, getting that procedure or process in place, it doesn't matter as poetry of which kind: Ginsberg-like or ornate prose, or if it's highly mannered postmodernist. It doesn't really trouble me. I can leave my own self behind at a certain level and just address what's there in front of me. So I think writing is about technique, but it's not about 'style'. It's about actually getting into what you're doing. It's like any other form of art. You have to learn how to do what you're doing as best as you can do it.

AT: *Do you feel any diffidence in dealing with other forms; perhaps you haven't practiced yourself, like novel writing?*

GD: Humility, I think. *[AT: Brief chuckle]* It never fails to amaze me how anyone could write a novel.

AT: *I was actually going to ask you have you been tempted by these other forms at all. Lots of people try different things, will write plays, will write essays, and will write novel and stories. You seem to be determined to be a poet.*

GD: When I was in my late teens, early twenties, I wrote a couple of short stories, but they were terrible and I realized that that was that. I still have one around but I mean it just wasn't there. And when I was in college as an undergraduate I wrote two plays which were translated into Irish and I worked in the translation into Irish. And they were put on stage at different [venues]. I was a member of Cumann Dramaiochta, so I actually did different things along that and I loved that. If I was ever going to do anything other than write poems and the occasional essay, it would be to write a play.

AT: *As well as being involved in creative writing, you also have had an academic training. You've done postgraduate work and you've written as a critic. Do you find any clash between the freedoms of the imagination that you have as a poet with the fact that you have to follow very definite disciplines within the academic community? Is there a tension there as well?*

GD: There is always going to be a tension between a teacher's life and a writer's life, a poet's life. And I think wrong to suggest that there cannot be. It's how you handle the tension, the obligations of being an academic, of looking after students, and the increasing administration that goes along with it, this can short circuit, and sometimes overload you. But then you have the benefit of age and you can pull back and reshuffle the pack again. There was a period of time I think I was probably doing too much, too many other things and I started to drift away from where I felt I should be as a writer. It sounds a little bit over the top, but I think you begin to have psychic problems as a result of that, fall into ill health if writing is such an essential part of your nature that suddenly, or over a period of time, you become remote from it. You're going to get into trouble. Age does give you that value whereby you can, as I said, reshuffle the pack and see what needs to go and what doesn't. And I'm now thankfully reaching that stage. I think it's an arrogant assumption that because someone is a teacher, or a doctor, or a bus driver, or whatever, that in some way they are less a writer for doing those other things. I mean I always come back to the magnificent William Carlos Williams and the notion of his being a doctor and you just look at the shelves of William Carlos

Williams' books and the number of people he looked after. This was a man who was living in the world. In our culture there is still a kind of a *caché,* or nervous tic, that if you're a real writer, you have to be full time and that those of us who are engaged in some other kind of activity, be it academic, civil service, or some professional engagement, that we're not quite making the mark. Now I don't know what that reflects in our culture because it certainly doesn't happen anywhere else in the world that I know of. The tension that you mentioned can be a fruitful one, but you have to be alert to when it's becoming a burden.

AT: *And how is the creative process for you? Where does a poem begin? Does it start with an image; does it start with an idea, with a shape? And how do you then manage to hammer it into poem? You gave an example of 'The Clock on a Wall of Farringdon Gardens, August 1971'* [The Lundys Letter 1985] *Do you have any other examples like that of a poem that started somewhere, and then you worked on it and it came to fruition?*

GD: There are two 'ways' that poems come to me. I wait for poems. I don't go looking for them, because I feel that you need really to have the radar on. Most of the time, I don't know what I'm doing, until I hear something. There was a line that kept on going round and round and round in my head in the early 80s, 'I was like a man walking in a circle, no one else was near.' [*'Solstice'*, The Lundys Letter]. I didn't know where the line came from but it kept at me and at me and at me and the poem came out of that. When I moved to Galway I moved out of the city centre and into the countryside. Looking out the back window I could see a bath and the bath was in commonage where there were a couple of 'lakes' around it. It was an extraordinary sight. The bath was there. It was a white enamel bath and of course the bath was there for the cattle. But when you looked at it from my point of view it was like a Magritte installation, that here was a bath in the field. I mean it was quite an extraordinary kind of image and a poem came from that [*'A Story'*, Sunday School, 1991]. So without being dogmatic about it, poems come, as far as I can see in my work, from two clear sources: an image, which just will not go away—something that I see and that intrigues me. Or something that I hear and the poem writes itself.

AT: *And how long does it take between seeing the bath to hear your phrase...*

GD: Oh, forever!

AT: *and writing it down?*

GD: It takes time between what reality gives you and how the poem happens. For me, if I rush it, the 'karma' will go, the magic will go. But if I hold onto it and have the confidence to hold onto it, it'll come back and come back and come back, and that's when I know I'm onto something.

AT: *Do you keep notebooks for this purpose?*

GD: I do. All my work, I write out and then reluctantly move on to the computer. And that's the moment when I actually see how it looks on the page, so the visual thing takes over. But I mean, basically, all the stuff is in there in journals...

AT: *And do you show your poetry to any poetic friends? Do you show them to anybody beforehand? Or do they come directly from you and say that's it?*

GD: When I was younger, in my 20s and 30s, I used to show poems to a couple of friends, one of whom is a very fine poet, Gerard Fanning and we used to argue the toss over this or that. And then a little bit later, I would send the book in a draft to a couple of other friends and ask what they thought of it. When you get older if you can't trust your own judgment you might as well not be doing it. I have my regular arm wrestling with the publisher, Peter Fallon. Peter is a very alert editor, one of the best in the country. And he will identify any looseness or strain in the work. So that when you know it's ultimately going to go to Peter, you just wait and then you have the extraordinary moment when you go through the entire manuscript. So he has taken over from the intimacies of sending it to chums.

AT: *How do you feel about critics? Have critics been kind to you? Or do you think that critics really haven't a clue as what they're talking about, with regard to your work?*

GD: I've been fairly lucky. I can't complain. The work that I've published over the last 25 years has been well received in the main.

But I think that what has happened in the last five or ten years is a cause for concern—that poetry is slipping down the critical list in so far as reviewers, and critical receivers of the material in the media, are becoming less interested. Needless to say, the volume of work coming out now is hard to filter. I'm quite relaxed about how my stuff is treated 'out there'. At the same time, on a wider front, I think that there's trouble ahead in so far as poets and their work are becoming less regarded by the critical media. Take Ireland: the number of magazines that used to be there in the 60s and 70s has narrowed and narrowed, so there's now only two or three. The space that they're devoting is going to creative writing, which is fair enough, to poems being published or short stories, and not to reviewing; which is fair enough. I know who's 'out there' reading me. I don't know them individually, but I have an idea who's there and how well the books sell. The contemporary world of marketing and so on, it's a different business and for this particular poet, for me, I'm not that involved in it. I do the occasional public reading, but I think the book has to look after itself.

AT: *How do you see the future for yourself? I mean, you're obviously writing all the time, you're determinedly doing your work as a poet. Do you have any sort of long term view you really want to write about this or that? Or is it you still wait for inspiration or just depends on what's going to happen?*

GD: It all depends. It all depends on what's going to happen. And I have never set myself objectives as a poet; I needed to get from *here* to get to *there*. I'm working on a new collection. And I'd like to bring together all the work from the late 70s to the book, *Lake Geneva*, which came out earlier this year [2003], into one book, have it all shaped and coherent.

AT: *Would you rewrite those poems if you were...?*

GD: Yeah, I'm doing a bit of that cutting and pasting, if you know what I mean. There are wee bits and pieces here and there which I'm uncomfortable with, so I'm snipping them. I'm a cutter. I'm an editor-down. I don't go the other way. So I'm bringing this towards what I hope will be the core of my work from my 20s to my late 50s. And in a funny kind of way, I feel that's a period of my life over. I don't know why. I hope that more books will come, but I feel there's a kind of coherence and symmetry to that 25-30 odd years and that I want to go on. I want to challenge myself more. I want to try different kinds of writing as a poet. I want to churn things up a bit. I suppose if there's one thing that runs through my work it is a kind of restlessness. Once I feel that things are settled I get anxious. I want to move on. And I think I've got to that stage now.

AT: *And in the far and distance future when people look back, how do you think you'll be remembered, as a poet?*

GD: Oh dear. I'd be happy if two things were registered. That I tried to write out of a community, i.e. the northern Protestant community, the Belfast Protestant community, and revealed their world with respect and the kind of justice which had not really been accrued to them before in many ways, that their experience had been trivialized or caricatured or stereotyped. And there's a side of my work which I think comes out of that. And I would like it if that was registered or recognized. But that's in the lap of the gods. The other thing is, that I would hope that the work would be read and understood, because I think there's a kind of humour in the work. And all too often reviewers are somewhat po-faced about it. And I like the notion that the kind of ironies and the shocks and the jokes, I hope they're going to be read and seen more in the future, than they are now. But as I just said, that's in the lap of the gods. When you bring those two things together, the northern Protestant thing and the other stuff I'm talking about, I hope that the design of the work, imaginatively and artistically, is appreciated as well.

AT: *Well, you've certainly been very illuminating. It's been great talking to you and we wish you all luck with those great new books that will be coming in the future. Thank you very much Gerry.*

GD: Thanks, Alan.

The Way It Is

with Nicholas Allen
& David Gardiner

NA: *We're here to talk about your collected essays,* The Proper Word. *What do you think is the proper word?*

GD: If there's a centre to this collections it's the link—the crossover—the 'proper' relationship to the intersection between writing, creativity, the imagination and the impact and influence of politics. The proper word is the relationship, the protected relationship or the filter between the freedom of the imagination to rove, and at the same time to engage, at some level, with politics and the here and now. So, I suppose the proper word is the adequate word or sufficient word, the way in which the imagination can negotiate the present.

NA: *Do you think that negotiation is different between poetry and prose?*

GD: Yes. I think that prose is much more logical and much more open. Poetry is evasive and tends to be deeper, a less forthcoming art form. And that's not to say that there aren't writers who in their poetry strike 'prosaic' positions, if you like. I mean great poets like Brecht—the sharpness of his poems that I've read in

English record a kind of upfront confrontation, but they still create this disarming poetic. And there are other poets who don't go there; they actually go away from the whole social and political world and it's a deflected look. And one of the poets a lot of people are talking about today, Elizabeth Bishop, seem to me to be that kind of evasive poet even though what she's evading comes back around into the poem.

NA: *You talk about this division, I suppose, between the logicality of prose and the evasiveness of poetry. But whenever I read your prose there is an element of poetry in it. Do the two things speak to you when you write about poets?*

GD: I think that *The Proper Word* is a poet's criticism; it's not a critic's criticism, if you know what I mean. A lot of the writers I've been drawn to, I've been drawn to as a poet. But I'm very interested in ideas as well; ideas about art, ideas about political propriety and so on. So maybe there is a sense in which *The Proper Word* is actually trying to work out a personal rationale concerning the relationship between poetry and prose, if nothing else.

DG: *If I could return to semi-ancient history, back to your first moments in Galway. There's a wonderful 'prose-poem' where you talk about coming into Eyre Square. In this piece, 'Beauty' [published in* Vacuum*] you talk about asking for directions to the Imperial Hotel. What I'm thinking of is that moment where poetry and prose intersect, and I recall in our first meetings and the impact that* The New Younger Irish Poets *was making—that critical eye towards making that sufficient gesture—that your place is not just within Irish poetry, but of finding a European place, a place also within the [European] continent. If you jog your memory a little bit back to that moment of* The New Younger Irish Poets, *coming from your early critical training and establishing yourself, if you want to even refer to it as The Academy, and how you charted the critical ground with* Krino, *as well—you can view that critical impact, your intersection, as a way that bridges poetry and prose, politics and writing.*

GD: Well, let me think about that now. The first edition of *The Younger Irish Poets* came out in 1982 and the second barely ten years later in 1991. What I was trying to do was to make an 'anthological' statement about how I saw Irish poetry. I couldn't see it then, and I still can't see it now, as being in anyway divided between north and south. I thought that view was a rather understandable shorthand for other things. When I edited the first *Younger Irish Poets* it struck me that there were a lot of younger poets writing in the Republic in the 1970s who weren't being identified or recognized, like Paul Durcan, and others, such as Matthew Sweeney, who seemed to be slipping off the radar. So I wanted to make a kind of an audit of how I was reading things then. And you're absolutely right, there's a cluster of essays published around that time, which were 'probes', trying to find out what contemporary Irish writing actually was all about, particularly poetry. And as I went further on I read a lot and spent a lot of time in the loft, as it was, of Kenny's Bookshop in Abbeygate Street in Galway, going through pamphlets and all this fugitive material, which hadn't really before been brought together. Then between '82 and '91 there was a change in the whole 'system' of poetry in Ireland, it became more obviously professionalized, and I wanted to do another critical reading. Blackstaff asked me again and I said yes, I would do another reading or register of the situation and see how things had progressed, or not as the case may be. And at that stage it had almost become de facto that the northern poets had established a school and a critical mass, whereas the southern poets had become, in a sense, more integrated into the English literary scene and were being published in the UK. There was the huge appetite in America for Irish poetry with a capital I and P. So in a sense the argument had moved on, but it had always fascinated me, this notion about what constitutes a *national* tradition. I wasn't comfortable with the idea, and I'm not quite sure why I wasn't comfortable about it, but I always was intrigued; that you were, in some way, authorized to be an Irish writer because you were part of the *national* tradition. But what happens if you don't *feel* yourself to be part of that national tradition? Are you disenfranchised; disqualified? And as I was thinking about these things, I also started to think about my own background, which included way back, refugees. That led me to a different kind of exposure, a fascination with European writing. When I was in my teens I remember reading Dostoyevsky and being absolutely amazed by him; it was a shock to the very quick. Then you read all of it and become obsessive: everything by Turgenev, everything by Camus. But the more I read, the more I realized you could be provincial in Europe *and* yet be international, like Kafka! The need to be *defined* by a national tradition can actually be strengthening, at one time; but also limiting, at another. Certainly in the seventies and eighties any time I went outside the country and was introduced as an Irish writer, I was proud and pleased. But it developed into a kind of tic—it wasn't the *poetry* that mattered so much as the *Irishness* of the poetry. So, I became a bit uneasy about that. All these things entered into a big 'stew', and out of that you never know where you're going. I started to entertain the notion that it might be possible to rethink the whole notion of tradition through poetry. I wrote a couple of essays about this and the idea was to write a PhD about the Thirties generation who more or less took up the same kind of ideas—Beckett and so on—writers who talked very forcefully about the notion that the writer doesn't have any nationality or nation and is without brothers, or borders, but on his own. I liked that notion, but it goes against the grain of the popular sense of Irish writing that's very much there today. Looking back on it now, it was an instinctive thing that took on a kind of backdated intellectual rationale. At the same time these notions were fueled by an uncertainty with who *I* was, and where I was, in the eighties. It was a very, very dark time, a very dark time. When you think back to the hunger strikes, the assassinations and the sectarianism, it was a really grim time. I was trying to find, where is the light in all of this, where's the air, where is the oxygen. I was looking to writers who had gone through similar experiences. The Italian poet I read a lot was Eugenio Montale. I read about Lorca, writers who had negotiated sectarian or civil issues, such as we were experiencing in Ireland: that's where a lot of the work started to bubble up.

DG: *You can see all this in some of your collections. The division I see in* Sunday School, *where there are the political poems, which are located, mostly Northern, with interiors—mantelpieces, domestic interiors—and then poems such as 'A Story' or 'Straws in the Wind', which are set in Galway and the West, while with the more recent collections, such as* The Morning Train *and* Lake Geneva, *it seems we are looking towards Europe, working towards assimilation.*

GD: I never felt that I was a *political* writer. I've only written one clearly political poem, 'A Question of Covenants', which is about

Northern Protestantism. A lot of the poems, (and again this wasn't deliberate, it was just the way it came out), carry the history and the politics in domestic detail, metaphors like clocks and windows and the bric-a-brac of a lifestyle; almost radioactive with a culture, rather than actually taking on political dimensions. I just found that this sort of portraiture seemed to have political potency. And it wasn't simplifying a culture; it was *rendering* a culture, in some sense. You're right, *The Lundys Letter* and *Sunday School* were partly about these things, which culminated in *Heart of Hearts*. I've often thought of these three books as forming a unit. The first book, *Sheltering Places*, was heavily influenced by a young man's shock at the world that he had known growing up falling apart. I don't think I knew exactly how to express it—the sense in which the world that we had known, a very useful world and an entertaining world, in the sixties, had suddenly gone. As Larkin says, at an age when self-importance seemed natural, events cut us relentlessly down to size. And we all had to readjust, and then I left. When you go, as you probably know, there is a sense of guilt. And there's no better place in the world to really feel that than in Ireland, even though you're not actually so far away. I was back and forward to Belfast all the time. But there was the sense that you had left 'your' people behind. I mean it was ridiculous, looking back, ludicrous! But there was the intensity of the time and there was a sense in which not only had I left, I was supposed to go to England, which would have been understandable, but I went instead to the West of Ireland, which was unforgivable. Nobody was saying this upfront, but there was a sense in which I had 'betrayed'. But those early books—*The Lundys Letter, Sunday School* and *Heart of Hearts*—always seemed in my mind to form a coherent group. And then it begins to break up towards the end of *Heart of Hearts*, and the move into *The Morning Train*. Parts of the poems in *Heart of Hearts* link in with *The Morning Train* and *Lake Geneva* and what I'm writing now. It's like those interlinked rings that magicians have, joined together: how do you break them apart? I don't quite know how they fit together, but they do.

NA: *The image I have more is of the bits and pieces of crates and finding all the different pieces of it in 'Vertigo'* [The Morning Train]. *It strikes me that when you travel, write and publish you are gathering up bits from that past as well. When you talk about having left there seems to be a kind of measured sense of engagement with bits that are still there. I mean you have an interest in the North still that, say, I don't have. And you still have a commitment and a belief in the place that I don't have.*

GD: I don't know where that comes from but you're absolutely right. I think that notion of being a collector is probably true even though I don't 'collect' anything as such; I'm sort of rummaging around in bits and pieces of the past. I actually had shunned everything to do with home in the seventies. I still had a very strong sense of it and a very strong sense that—how should I express this now?—a very strong sense that justice had not been done. And now I think even more so that that sense of justice not being done is, in terms of those people who experienced the last thirty years, got nothing out of it, but whose lives were, in many ways, if not destroyed—almost 3,000 of them were—that a sense in which the culture and the life that they lived was deeply contaminated by violence. But I'm not obsessed by it. I see the North in terms of a wider scale of things. And I think if we can understand what happened in the North we actually get an insight into human frailty and universal experiences: Rwanda, Kosovo, the whole European experience going back to the Second World War, as in Germany, the notion of racism in contemporary society here and in Britain. Northern Ireland is very dear to me emotionally, well maybe not Northern Ireland, but Belfast. But I see it as a microcosm of a much wider condition, and it doesn't matter where you would be in the world, or where I would be, I would still have that sense that Northern Ireland, that Belfast is like a keyhole through which I see history and read history and the repressed elements of that too are fascinating: the issues of minorities, refugees who kept quiet. I'm just rereading Brian Moore's *The Emperor of Ice-Cream*. The Jewish family that's in that novel is fascinating, but perhaps veers towards the stereotypical—these are issues that are very potent today, the extent to which a minority is given voice and acceptance by the wider civic society. So I don't see my fascination with Belfast as being anything other than a need to understand what went wrong. I'm not a number cruncher; not (I hope) obsessed with traffic spotting about who's right and who's wrong. It's the actual human issues, the universal issues that underpin it that have fascinated me, imaginatively and critically. But it's not where the real drive of my writing rests; it rests in the small fragments, on the coasts and on the windfall beaches you're talking about.

ND: *The question then is how you have found these far places in Ireland today—you have always had an interest in Eastern Europe. I wonder have you any thoughts on Ireland finally meeting Eastern Europe in a way you did imaginatively twenty years ago—physically, socially and culturally here it is. Perhaps it's different than you might have thought it would be.*

GD: Absolutely different. In the early-mid '90's I was touring around giving readings and talks through what used to be Eastern Europe, talking about the enlargement of Europe, talking about Ireland as a model, as a paradigm of a small society, an old traditional society and a modernist project of 'moving forward' into this new enlarged Europe, so on, so forth. But nobody expected what would happen to happen. No one really thought that you could walk through Dun Laoghaire and not hear English spoken. I mean that is a huge transformation but we are absolutely leaderless in regards to this *politically*. So it's fascinating to see that what was in people's heads, back in the late eighties-early nineties, has now actually *happened*, but not the way people thought it would. I'm not so sure that any society has really worked out politically the implications of such economic and cultural change. Certainly in terms of our field of literature it has significant implications. That was why I was so taken by Hugo Hamilton's wonderful *The Speckled People* because I thought it broke first into new territory, through the story of his father and mother. It was something that I had been trying to do in scattered poems here and there—to go back into the other histories that underpin Irish society, or hear these histories that have now broken through, and they've broken through at an extraordinary level because there's been this constant flow of Europe into Ireland. I mean it was all very nice to say that we were Irish and European. Now Ireland *is* European. I don't know how much the Holocaust is being taught in schools in Ireland, I don't know, for instance, how much history of Poland is being taught in schools in Ireland. The militarism of the Hapsburg dynasty, I don't know how much that's being taught—the history of the *peoples* of Europe. There is a real possibility and potentiality to realign our histories now, not through the Anglophobic past but through Europe, which is much more powerful. This is not to say we should diminish the obvious legacy of 'Britishness' in Ireland, the history of that imperial project, and vice versa. But we can actually start to think of ourselves as genuinely

European. So what happens if you take that Anglo bit out of our mind, if you dislodge the British obsession. Where does that leave us? We keep hearing, 'Oh, we're not obsessed with England, or Britain'. I'm not so sure about that; the Anglo obsession of the Irish still presides. With Europe it actually gives a genuine way of realigning the whole thing.

NA: *I suppose that was arguably part of the Good Friday Agreement, part of the archipelago of the islands. The other thing that comes to mind is that since you were in America recently and you spent some time in Boston, the heart of Irish-America, is that actually going to go, as Ireland becomes European again? Is it American too?*

GD: In this post-modern world, you can be just about whoever you want to be, so it's not a question of one thing or the other. The impact of Iraq globally and in Ireland is interesting, as is its impact on the Irish relationship with America. It's a questionable one now. Even though this is a very close family relationship, I know that when I was in America and was asked to publicly comment upon how I thought about Iraq and American involvement, I felt I couldn't express a view because I was a guest. I know that there was and there is a very deep-seated anxiety about American intentions under this current administration. And that might have an impact in relationship to Ireland's America, but people can't be under any illusions. American military might underpins our freedom. We can quibble about their politics and the terror that's going on in Iraq but America still is the banker for European freedoms in many ways. They pay for it. So the relationship between Ireland and Britain is one thing. Between Ireland and Europe is another. But there's something very deep-seated and ambiguous about our relationship with America. I have been surprised by the extent to which writers in America have felt so angry about their powerlessness. Certainly the ones I've met and talked with felt that whatever they said was like dropping a penny down a well.

NA: *I wonder if this connects to something you said earlier about your idea of the North and the South as being a cypher. Because I sometimes think that when people talk about America and Ireland in the cultural sense they are critical. But Irish capital wouldn't survive but for the American model. I mean that's the difference. It's just business. Europe is a cypher for intellectual life. Coffee in Paris, you know. In a way that kind of North/South divide of the area, industrial versus cultural, replicated itself in a curious way in other cultural relations.*

GD: It has. The civic nature of European society is under threat in Ireland now, the social partnership. If you look at a recent reading of the top twenty medical systems, Ireland is second from the bottom, France is at the top because there is this obsession or this care in France, whatever you may think about the pomposity of other elements of that society. But the civic nature of the society, its health and so on, is important. Now I think that's under pressure in Ireland. We tend to pick up more of our social configuration not from America, not from Europe, but from Britain. I think that's still the case. We replicate the British model more than the American and European, and I daresay that's historical. The way we are going, in terms of structural changes in the academy, is not in relationship to America. We're more or less starting to mix them together but based more around the *English* model of strategic reports and trying to create a corporate environment in the university, modeled on big business. And that's all very well in America where big business seriously underwrites the university with huge endowments for the humanities as well as the sciences; it's not so much the case in Britain where the social underpinning of universities by the state is steadily shrinking and students take out loans to get their way through college—a shocking development under the British *Labour* Government. I don't think we know where we are, and I think that's true culturally and politically. But then that could also be read as being a historical moment. And underneath it, you have the real, hardcore political issues of race hatred and terrorism, bubbling up and governments getting it absolutely wrong, like the attack on the two young Muslims in London a couple weeks back. Intelligence not being correct, the riots in France. If you were to take a bird's eye view of where we are maybe we're at a rerun of the 1930's. If you wanted to be pessimistic about it, you could see this as being the beginnings of another war. I don't think that's going to happen, but these are difficult times, and the real irony is that it's also the best of times. Ireland has 'never had it so good'. Yet in terms of writing, there's been a steady but inevitable erosion of its cultural *authority* as writing. Many writers go ahead and do their business as they should do, writing their poems or plays and novels. What's happened is that the authority of literature is being sidelined more and more as the carnival associated with writers and 'being a writer', draws more and more media attention. The Beckett celebrations were excellent but at no point along the way were his criticisms voiced, or his satirical comments about the relationship of culture and public access. The kind of adoration of the financial world, the corporate world, is all very fine—there are pages and pages and pages about it in the newspaper every day—all very well, but in the past all this business would have been a small note in the back of the newspaper. Now it dominates. So what? These things happen, things change. But the notion that golf is of such vast importance strikes me as being a metaphor of where we are politically. I know you like golf.

DG: *And so did Beckett.*

GD: Yeah, yeah, I know, I mean...[laughter]... I think this might seem a contradiction to everything I've said; maybe it is. The only way you can really rebutt something is by presenting people with facts and information. The essays in *The Proper Word* about poets, such as Charlie Donnelly and Thomas Kinsella, are basically saying: 'this is their lives, this their work. Now, what do you think?' Maybe 'rebuttal' is too upfront a term, but the book is an anthology; a statement of a person who's not here anymore and thirty years of his work. Looking back at all of this I can remember when I wrote the essays and how long it took me to write them and so on. I'm thrilled that the book is coming out, because it makes a statement of intent, if not of actual critical achievement. It summarizes other possibilities, another reading, that's all. I like things to be open and people to have choice. In a way 'consensus' is a phony word unless you have *all* the cards on the table. The book's a little contribution towards that sense of openness and availability. Let people make up their own minds and decide what they like. People should have all kinds of different literary experiences. And I think if this book does anything it might say, 'what about this? Did you try that?'

NA: *Does that sense of experiment extend to poems you're working on at the moment in terms of forms, such as the work in* Vacuum?

GD: *Vacuum* in Belfast asked me to write a couple of things for their newspaper. I don't know why or how, but each piece fell out as a kind of 'prose-poem'. And in 2004 RTE asked me to write a commemorative piece for Bloomsday, myself and several other writers. I wrote my piece in the voice of Molly Bloom, as if she was living in Dublin today. I then wrote other pieces—"The Fair," "Beauty," and "Little Clouds". They're poetic fragments—modeled on what you'd see in a Fellini film. When I was in college I watched a lot of Italian movies, they fascinated me, so I suppose these are little Thank-You's. I'm interested in the structure of memory; how things are represented in the here and now. It's not just a question of reciting the past; it's about understanding how the past lives on, if it can?

NA: *In your most recent poems there's a recurrence of the upper rooms in Dun Laoghaire and the windows and domestic spaces that is beginning to remind me of another poet, Thomas Kinsella, who wrote of Baggot Street and its transformation, from his upper room and that world of possibilities. It's not your aesthetic to write with precise models in mind, but Kinsella does seem to me similarly situated as he was observing and watching an Ireland being transformed, as you are now in Dun Laoghaire, and then on to the continent.*

GD: I haven't thought of the connection with Kinsella but you're the second one to have mentioned it. John McAuliffe also mentioned it reviewing *The Morning Train* in the *Irish Times*. And I never made the connection. But the point you make is the case. Why that should be I have no idea because I haven't thought of myself as being connected with Kinsella, other than my understanding as a teacher of his work. I've never seen it present in my writing. But if the comparison's there, so be it. Certainly the sense of moving up to a higher space is in Kinsella, there's no doubt about that. But there was also a book I read when I was quite young that had a big impact on me, called *The Poetics of Space*, philosophizing about *bric-a-brac*—cubby-holes, attics and the like. I grew up in a house full of women and I think that in that particular house and that particular time, there was a place for everything; everything in that place had its own significance. As a young boy I absorbed it into myself without knowing it or thinking about it. So these items—furniture, clocks, and mirrors—became important, all that kind of theatre of women's lives that surrounded me. I felt I was a kind of scene changer, moving in and out, observing them. It almost became like a figure in a Sartre short story. It was physical, it wasn't intellectual, but then when I discovered this book it was a bit of a shock, I knew exactly what Bachelard was talking about. He takes you down into cellars, we didn't have a cellar. I mean the cupboards, the attics, (I lived in the attic), that was where I physically lived—where my bedroom was. I had a window that looked over Belfast. There was an unused fireplace, there was a tallboy, and there were these tea chests, full of song and sheet music. So all of this was surrounding, so when I read Bachelard's book it was like reading my own history, my own biography. But I didn't think it meant anything until he said, well these things do actually have significances.

DG: *This makes sense with the sort of unreality when the spaces go from the inside to the out. More than once you have used the term 'de Chirico streets' ['Siesta', Lake Geneva] and looking at the outside as these sort of shadowy presences, but not shadowy in sense of foreboding usually, but shadowing in a sense of…*

GD: *[finishing David's sentence]* That's the way it is.

DG: *…of things.*

GD: If I wanted to be anything other than what I am, I would have been a painter, because I love trying to get the angles right, to see. I'm not all that interested in colour but the shadow of the angle, as light becomes dark. All these lines that separate one thing from another but are linked together. It's very much down to the fact that I grew up in a society where (physically) light was important because when you live in the North the sun's benign. It's very important. For long stretches of the year you spend a lot of the time in darkness, going to school in the morning it's dark and by four o'clock coming home it's dark. So *light* is important. The light of lamps on streets, shop windows, the light flooding out, I have very strong recollections of all that. So maybe it all fed into the poetry as well.

NA: *You've spoken about foreboding, the shadows. Yet the other part of the geography we have talked about always being there in Belfast, Galway or in Dublin is the sea, and the sea to you is sort of a beautiful medium, isn't it? I get the idea of the painterly movement, but also that one that I love in 'The Minos Hotel' [10, The Morning Train], is the calling that there is somewhere else?*

GD: Yes indeed. I think I know where that comes from, and I hope this doesn't sound like psychobabble, but we had family in London, so we used to go back and forth quite a bit, my mother and I and my sister. We used to get the ferry from Belfast and go across to England and take the train down to London.

NA: *Did you go to Liverpool?*

GD: No, it was Crewe. One of the images that struck me when I was very small was when we walked up the gangplank looking down at the gap between the ship and the quay and seeing the engine of the ferry starting to churn. It had an extraordinary affect on me that I remember very clearly to this day—the sense that I was on the gangway between two different things, between the land and the sea with the ship sitting on it. It was both thrilling and frightening at the same time. When the ship takes off out of Belfast it reverses out, no, it reverses in and reverses back out again. So you have this strange moment where you're on the ship and you see the lough on either side of you. It's brilliant. And then you leave the lough and its embrace and you're out in the open sea. And that can be both exhilarating but also a little frightening for a kid. I think I carried that with me so I love being on the sea, but I'm also a little bit anxious about it. If you grew up in the North you're never too far from the coast, the sea; in Belfast I was ten minutes, six minutes away. We used to take a house in Bangor (by the sea), and stay in a house in Portstewart (by the sea), a house in Portrush, (by the sea). We would have had vertigo if we had gone too far inland! Everywhere we went was by the coast. When I went to college it was by the coast, when I moved to Galway it was by the coast, when I moved to Dun Laoghaire, it was by the coast. It was just like a calling, you know. When I was in Switzerland I pretended that Lake Geneva was the coast because I didn't like the idea I was too far inland.

DG: *In Omaha, I'm desperate…I have to pretend the Missouri River is an ocean.* (Laughter). *At a reading once, someone asked you about the prevalence of foghorns in your work!*

GD: Oh yes?

DG: *That it's sort of calling out too. That's when I started thinking about those upper spaces that are occupied because in talking about where you lived as a child it seems it isn't a halfway point, but a calling out, answering a voice maybe.*

GD: I remember the foghorns, and the sirens for work. These sirens had been used to alert people to nightly raids or the possibility of bombing raids during the Second World War. I can hear those to this very day, the sirens of the shipyards. Belfast was *defined* by work. Its *raison d'etre* was industrial—customs, seasons, holidays, clocks—*everything* was defined by industry. So that if you're a young kid growing up in that environment you don't 'know' this because you don't know anything else. But what you do know is the sound of the sirens—people are at work by eight o'clock, but also nights, the sound of the foghorns. You can hear it; it's like owls hooting, you know, because there's fog on the lough. And that's both exciting, because you're sitting there in your attic bedroom, but it is also a bit spooky. It's got the Edgar Allen Poe feel about it. So the foghorn becomes like a siren call, like someone calling you away, and then you're not too far away from Homeric possibilities—you know that you're on the sea.

DG: *I want to follow up then about "night sounds,"—they're something that you write more about in the prose than in the poetry and that's sex, rock 'n roll, Belfast and how it fits together. You have written about popular music, rock 'n roll, the blues, jazz coming from Belfast, although it's only present, tangentially in the poems.*

GD: I just never found a way to adequately represent, or convincingly write a poem out of that world; the world of popular music and jazz, even though it was so important and still is. It's beginning to percolate through a little bit in the new poems. There are whiffs of it here and there. I don't want to make it sound funny and poetry is such a tough taskmaster. It's more difficult whereas I enjoy writing about it in prose, because it's easier that way. We nearly done? Let's say one or two final things about the book. Can I ask you both a question? The book finishes about 2002, or thereabouts, with the essay, 'History class'. Does it give a portrait of thirty years of Irish writing?

NA: *Definitely.* The Proper Word, *to me, is reportage. It's as if you came across a war-correspondence of a journalist who got caught up somewhere. And all this stuff had been put into a locker and then been discovered afterwards. There's an element of that which I like very much. It doesn't tell you what these things are.*

GD: It doesn't tell you what you *should* think these things are?

NA: *It reminds me a little bit more of your poems and I think you make the point in your 'Postscript' that these things 'just were'. What they should have been is up to the reader.*

GD: That's encouraging.

DG: *The criticism stands on its own as it always has, I think. Good criticism leads you towards the work as well. Sort of like weather forecasting so that if you enjoy being outside you don't get hooked on watching what's going to happen. There isn't a great deal of prediction happening, these are essays in the classical sense. I think it's very important, especially today when writers seem to be getting agents before they bring out their first publications. On the other hand, there are authors, especially of your [GD] generation who will perhaps be unknown because of the politics of publishing. They're going to be lost because so many readers look for divisions. Where does this writer fit? That's why Krino was such an important publication, and why keeping these essays as ideas before the self-discovering reader is important too.*

GD: That is why I find America so liberating because they relate there to what is Irish *and* European, the multiculturalism of writing; that *that* is in itself a defining characteristic of what it means to be Irish or should be. You have to at some point kick free and just be you. But there is openness in America, which hasn't really happened here, that our work is read by agenda, by niches, where does he or she fit in, and if you are against fitting in, readers and critics sometimes don't know where to put you. That's a problem.

NA: *When I think about* The Proper Word, *I think of a civic enterprise. There is an argument that the republican idea is freedom as a refusal to dominate.*

GD: That is exactly what I'm talking about.

III

POSTSCRIPT:

The War Next Door

It ends where it began, literally next door, in the house I moved to as a young boy in the Belfast of the 1950s. The terraced row was fairly typical late Victorian, not particularly graceful houses. What made the neighbourhood important, looking back over forty years, were the people who lived there. Next door there was an Austrian woman who had fallen in love with a dashing young Northern Irish soldier who had been stationed in Vienna at the end of WWII. She was an incredibly tall woman who dressed 'up'; she bred pedigree poodles and spoke with a very pronounced 'foreign' accent. Next door to this lady and her extremely quiet, civil servant husband, was a large family with whom I became very friendly; indeed, at one stage of my boyhood, I was almost a foster son of this family. They were a Catholic family, unlike my own, and I loved being with them. My mother did not mind, nor my grandmother, with whom I lived, and during the 1950s and 1960s, this little patch of Belfast—that terrace, the encircling avenues, main roads, that district—was my home. I knew it, as we say, like the back of my hand.

I count myself lucky to have been brought up in that particular place and time because from my boyhood, without actually knowing it then, I was experiencing difference; cultural diversity, as we would say now. The Catholic family became very much a part of our life. So too with the Austrian lady, who fascinated me, with her domestic rituals of thick rich coffee in little small cups and her strange mix of formality and vulnerability. A little later, in the mid Sixties, I also became very friendly with several Jewish families who lived in our immediate district. That cultural mix was healthy: there was a synagogue, delicatessen, and hairstylist— all part of the local fabric; it freed up the mind, maybe not in contemporaneous time but afterwards; later on.

It is important to state this as bluntly as possible, given what we now know was to happen in Belfast by the late 1960s and early 1970s, as the city turned into a bloody site of sectarian warfare and a struggle for political (and cultural) supremacy and retribution. Indeed the particular area of North Belfast which I am describing became in more recent times, one of the most bitter interface areas of sectarian conflict with Protestant families accusing Catholic families of seeking to 'ethnically cleanse' them from the area. Catholic families, on the other hand, counter with accusations of constant sectarian attacks from loyalist gangs.

The history of Belfast since its emergence as an industrial city in the 1840s was very much wrapped up with the economic destiny of Britain. The city drew into its constricted low-lying basin hundreds of thousands of unskilled and skilled workers from the rural Irish hinterlands, from Scotland and from England. With the foundation of the Irish Free State in 1922 and the partition of Ireland the substantial Catholic minority remaining inside the new Northern Irish "Protestant" state felt isolated and marooned within a hostile political culture. The failure to seriously address and integrate that Catholic minority ultimately lead to the eruption of 'The Troubles', a thirty year conflict which left 3000 dead and countless thousands maimed both physically and psychically, primarily in Northern Ireland but also further in the Republic, in Britain and in Europe. (There has to be a lesson here for our globalised world of the 21st century).

Against this bloody backdrop, the cultural mix that I mentioned as being a part of my own upbringing in Belfast has been largely destroyed. In its place emerged 'No Go' areas that eventually mutated into a patchwork landscape of exclusionist districts, either

Protestant or Catholic, loyalist or nationalist, literally ring-fenced against each other with the grotesquely named Peace Lines demarcating a divided city that in turn reflected a divided province. Today Northern Ireland lives in a kind of cultural flux with many of its people living their lives in a constantly contested battle of flags and emblems, mutually excluding one another, either physically or symbolically. It is a war of nerves now as much as anything else.

So one can see the Northern Ireland situation, or the Belfast situation, as a political analogue to what was to happen throughout eastern Europe by the time the communist states crumbled and the refrigerated ethnic tensions resurfaced without any powerful civic intervention and mediation.

Paramilitary or para-political forces on the ground parcelled up parts of Belfast as the overarching political system stalled. The fall out, in terms of law and order, drug problems, localised power struggles, political patronage and favour, is the evening news bulletins.

What we are currently seeing in Northern Ireland is the latest protracted attempt to restore some form of accountable democracy to a people who do not know how to imagine what each other have actually been through, during the past thirty years. Behind the parliamentary language of compromise and mutual understanding there is still a huge gulf of mistrust and ignorance upon which prey the bigots and violence junkies. It is also a minuscule version of what could take place worldwide if multicultural democratic governments don't seriously tackle the ideological and economic impulses of fundamentalism. For much of this intense local political gamesmanship at local level has an obvious, direct and critical bearing upon the template of possibilities, which we call, idealistically, Europe'.

I was schooled in British history; to most of my generation WWII was still part of our psychic and social landscape, whether we liked it or not. The public figures of that time, the names of battles, the sense of war and destruction in countries and cities the names of which we heard of in school, television and in film, filled up my mind and my imagination. Yet it was a 'Europe' in fundamental ways distant. As I've said earlier, it started to take on a much more personal meaning when I saw in the mid Sixties a photograph in The *Observer* newspaper (commemorating the beginning of the war) of a young Jewish boy being rounded up by the Gestapo, his arms raised, his large cap seeming too big for his frightened face. Somewhat later I followed with fascination developments in (as it then was) Czechoslovakia and wrote a poem in homage to Jan Palach, the young student who set himself on fire in St Wenceslas Square in Prague in protest at the Russian invasion and the ensuing closure of the borders between Czechoslovakia and the outside world.

Many years later I met a Czech émigré on a family holiday in Santorini. His sense of where he came from and what he belonged to exposed my own frail knowledge of where this place 'Europe' actually was and is, while the map he drew on a napkin is embossed forever in my mind.

I also started to probe my own family background and discovered that on one side of the family, my mother's side, we had been refugees who arrived in Ireland during the persecution of the Huguenots; my maternal great grandmother's people had also arrived in Belfast, bearing the surname 'Quartz.' Alongside this mixture there was on my maternal grandfather's side, well-established roots in Fermanagh in the northwest of Ireland while my own father's people had connections with the borders of England and Wales. This all amounted to a kind of cultural dispensation, a cultural coding.

So when I started to think about what 'European' identity meant, it occurred to me that we share this kind of multicultural familial past and that it will in turn become increasingly more common if present patterns of migration continue in the years ahead throughout Europe, and none more so than in Ireland.

None of this consciousness would have come through formal schooling. It is random and unstructured, related more to chance— an Austrian neighbour next door—as much as genealogy. But probe ever so lightly into most families, and one will find the variable figure, the different strain, influence or background. The problem is when this difference is locked away, either literally or metaphorically, in the (political, economic or cultural) interests of one exclusive dominant identity: the prison of fundamentalism. What happens then can become shocking beyond belief, as WWII demonstrated and as the end of the twentieth century showed in Bosnia, Kosovo and elsewhere; horrifying measures of ethnic cleansing just do not disappear.

Now much enlarged and enlarging Europe is becoming smaller than it ever was before. A matter of three or four hours could take me from my front door in Dublin to Belgrade or what had been the cauldron of Kosovo. The proximity is important because we have to imagine a time when the reconstructed democracies of former Yugoslavia, Albania, and Romania will be themselves part of Europe, alongside Poland, Slovenia and the Czech and Slovak republics. And what about the power keg that Turkey is becoming, a great culturally rich society edging ever closer to nationalist and religious extremism? Europe can be an extraordinary federation, as thousands of people cross borders and make new lives for themselves in other parts of Europe, bringing with them their different histories, customs, beliefs and cultures.

How we adjust to these changes will be the crucial defining test of political will in the 21st century. This is the template of possibility—of a European identity embracing all of Europe, not just its western flank, but its central and middle core and eastern periphery. No nation (super, or otherwise) will ever be called Europe and maybe its meaning resides in that very fact—of potentiality, ideal, and dream. People will discover other places not only on a couple of weeks holiday but as a re-imagining of all our histories and a new kind of inclusive historical consciousness can take root, if we prepare the ground for such a transformation.

In the final year of the last century, I was re-reading "Autumn Journal", Louis Mac Neice great poem, written in 1938. The poem, which is in 24 cantos, contains in its final canto the following lines, 'Let us dream it now/And pray for a possible land'. The lines haunted me, coming as they did just before the deluge of WWII. So sitting on the balcony of my hotel room I wrote 'Summer Journal', as a song to innocence and hope, a prelude to the new century, shadowed by the terrible scenes of the war happening next door, on our television screen:

SUMMER JOURNAL
for Brendan Kennelly

Through the porthole of a window
The blue muggy night is perforated
With the sound of foghorns.
Dogs answer each other back
And then it thunders again with spectacular effect.
The girls are sleeping in the cool apartment;

Shadows like planes cast over the lawn.
I'm in two minds between *Tender is the Night*
And the TV's mute hectic images
Which flash worldwide the breaking news
Of a hillside trek and scorched villages,
The bedecked impromptu briefing.

The ignominious beetle covers oceans of sand
But the man or woman who drifts
Into the sky, paragliding over our prone bodies—
Family groups setting up makeshift home,
Couples in their prime and past their prime,
The odd one alone stretched under the sun,

Where all are vulnerable, torn this way
And that, naked, flat, in repose from
The everyday, at sixes and sevens—
Is trussed and hooked to the speeding boat
And, cradled like a baby, looks down
Upon us all with far-seeing love and pity.

Palm doves and swallows in the apricot
And oleander, the cacophony
Of high season; poolside, *Mitteleuropa*
Tans and in silence observes a galleon
Take up the full of the bay.
The rosé goes down like mother's milk;

It's near ninety, best head for cover;
In the shade local dance music
Beats through the scratchy airwaves
To you on whichever island you stand:
'Let us dream it now,
and pray for a possible land.'

Bibliographical Note

POETRY COLLECTIONS:

Heritages (Isle of Skye: Aquila/Wayzgoose Press, 1976)

Blood & Moon (Belfast: Lagan Press, 1976)

Sheltering Places (Belfast: Blackstaff Press, 1978)

The Lundys Letter (Dublin: The Gallery Press, 1985)

The Water Table (Belfast: HU Publications, 1990)

Sunday School (Oldcastle: The Gallery Press, 1991)

Sheltering Places & Company (with images by Noel Connor)
 (Staffs: The Rudyard Press, 1993)

Heart of Hearts (Oldcastle: The Gallery Press, 1995)

The Morning Train (Oldcastle: The Gallery Press, 1999)

Lake Geneva (Oldcastle: The Gallery Press, 2003)

Sheltering Places: New Edition (Belfast: The Starling Press, 2008)

Points West (Oldcastle: The Gallery Press, 2008)

PROSE/CRITICISM:

How's the Poetry Going? Literary politics and Ireland today
 (Belfast: Lagan Press, 1991, 1993)

A Real Life Elsewhere (Belfast: Lagan Press, 1993)

False Faces: poetry, politics and place (Belfast: Lagan Press, 1994)

Against Piety: Essays in Irish poetry (Belfast: Lagan Press, 1995)

The Rest is History (Newry: The Abbey Press, 1998)

Stray Dogs and Dark Horses: selected essays on Irish writing and criticism
 (Newry: The Abbey Press, 2000)

The Proper Word: Collected criticism, Ireland, poetry, politics [ed. Nicholas Allen]
 (Omaha: Creighton University Press, 2007)

My Mother-City (Belfast: Lagan Press, 2007)

AS EDITOR/CO-EDITOR:

The Younger Irish Poets (Belfast: Blackstaff Press, 1982)

Across a Roaring Hill: the Protestant Imagination in Modern Ireland
   With Edna Longley (Belfast: Blackstaff Press, 1985)

The New Younger Irish Poets (Belfast: Blackstaff Press, 1991)

The Poet's Place: Essays on Ulster Literature and Society
   With John Wilson Foster (Belfast: Institute of Irish Studies, 1991)

Yeats: the poems, a new selection (Dublin: Anna Livia Press, 1993)

Ruined Pages: Selected Poems of Padraic Fiacc
   With Aodan MacPoilin (Belfast: Blackstaff Press 1994)

Krino: The Review 1986-1996, an anthology of modern Irish writing
   With Jonathan Williams (Dublin: Gill and Macmillan, 1996)

The Ogham Stone: an anthology of contemporary Ireland
   With Michael Mulreany (Dublin: Institute of Public Administration, 2001)

The Writer Fellow: an anthology
   With Terence Brown (Dublin: School of English, Trinity College, 2004)

The Night Fountain: Selected Early Poems of Salvatore Quasimodo
   in translation with Marco Sonzogni (Todmorden: Arc Publications, 2008)

High Pop: The Irish Times Column of Stewart Parker
   with Maria Johnston (Belfast: Lagan Press, 2008)

Earth Voices Whispering: Irish War Poetry, 1914-1945 (Belfast: Blackstaff Press, 2008)

AUTHOR'S WEBSITE:

www.gerald-dawe.net